EARLY CHILDHOOD EDUCATION SERIES

Millie Almy, Editor

STARTING SCHOOL
From Separation to Independence

A GUIDE FOR EARLY CHILDHOOD TEACHERS

Nancy Balaban
Bank Street College of Education

TEACHERS COLLEGE PRESS

Teachers College, Columbia University
New York and London

Published by Teachers College Press, 1234 Amsterdam Avenue, New York, N.Y. 10027

Grateful acknowledgment is extended to Elaine Wickens for the use of her photographs shown on pages 90–91. The rest of the photographs in the book were taken by the author.

Library of Congress Cataloging in Publication Data

Balaban, Nancy, 1928–
  Starting school.

  (Early childhood education series.)
  "Written as part of an Ed. D. dissertation for
New York University"—
  Bibliography: p.
  Includes index.
  1. Readiness for school.   2. School children—
Psychology.   I. Title.   II. Series.
LB1132.B34   1985   372.18   85-17264

ISBN 0-8077-2793-8 (pbk.)

Manufactured in the United States of America

98 97 96 95 94 93   9 8 7 6 5 4

To Dorothy

When my youngest daughter went to kindergarten an event took place that caused her daily distress. The teacher, it seems, put Willie in the coat room every morning because he cried for his mother. He was permitted back into the classroom when he stopped crying. Eventually he learned not to cry for his mother.

This book is written in the belief that other solutions to Willie's crying can be found.

Contents

Preface

Are you able to remember your first day at school?

Were you excited? Were you frightened? Were you sad?

Were you given a special pencil case or school bag? Did you wear a shiny new pair of shoes?

Can you call up in your mind's eye your family saying good-bye? Did you climb onto a yellow school bus with a pounding heart or a lump in your throat?

Do these remembrances of the first day of school come back with an aura of excitement? Do they come back with the sting of fear or worry? Do they come back with a bittersweet mixture of both?

Do you recall any small details of that school beginning long ago: a curtained kindergarten window, a sandbox, a strange child with curly hair, boxes of large crayons, a shiny linoleum floor, the teacher's face or voice? Are there any memories of standing by the nursery or kindergarten door, of trying out a new toy, of fighting back tears as your parent left? Are there flashes of newness or of strangeness?

Even though these memories are veiled by many years, they are often available to us as adults.

Beginning school is an important event.

This work about beginning school or group care is offered as an aid to teachers in the profound belief that this significant occasion can be a source of positive growth for everyone involved—teachers, children, and parents.

Acknowledgments

I wish to acknowledge the assistance and influence of a number of people.

This book was written as part of an Ed.D. dissertation for New York University. The chairperson of my sponsoring committee, Dr. Margot Ely, believed in and encouraged this work. Dr. Carol Millsom and Dr. Joanne Griffin, the other members of my committee, offered helpful, incisive comments. With the guidance of these three committee members, my project developed in breadth and scope.

Others added significantly to this project. Their dedication in completing my demanding questionnaires formed the first true test of my work. Their careful, critical, intelligent comments gave me confidence and guidance in the formation of these materials. I am deeply indebted to them. They are Ellen Galinsky, Dorothy Gross, Elisabeth Hirsch, William Hooks, Leigh Schuerholz, Lori Schneider, and Evangeline Ward. The comments of Erna Furman were insightful and rich. Editing done by Mary Allison was invaluable.

Many teachers who allowed me to take photographs in their classrooms contributed to this work. They are William Ayers, Sultana Christie, Amy Dombro, Ellen Friedman, Harriett Glassman, Judith Johnson, Valerie Kennedy, Susan Merrick, Lorelle Phillips, Jose Rivera, Leigh Schuerholz, Molly Sexton, Sr. Pat Dittmer, Marcine Weiner, Jane Rosenberg, and Zenola Williams.

Parents, though anonymous, were generous in answering my questionnaires. I want to acknowledge the help of Ellen Dublin, Jose Rivera, William Ayers, B.J. Richards, and Amy Dombro in distributing the questionnaires.

Four teachers who read this work and allowed me to interview them provided invaluable assistance. Vanessa Duncan, Dina Gabriel, Carmen Hawthorne, and Lois Melman willingly gave their time and thought.

Many students at Bank Street College contributed anecdotal records of children upon which I drew heavily. Their accuracy and careful recording were an important source.

Typing of the manuscript was done by Anne Goldstein with care and thought.

Finally, this project could not have been accomplished without the insights of Dr. Henriette Glatzer and the support, encouragement, and understanding of my husband, Richard Crohn.

This is when my Mommy left me.

Michele

1

Beginning School: How Does It Feel?

It is common fallacy to think that a young child who "does not mind" when his parents leave him or when he leaves them has coped well with the separation. The child who really copes well allows himself to miss the absent loved one, to feel sad, lonely and perhaps angry, and to express his feelings appropriately. (Furman, 1974, p. 16)

How does a young child feel going to school for the first time?
How do parents feel?
How do teachers feel on those first days?

Children, parents, and teachers all have a vast array of feelings about beginning school or group care.[1] A look at the nature of these feelings may sharpen our focus on this event.

WHAT MIGHT CHILDREN BE FEELING?

Separation from parents or a primary caregiver frequently makes young children unhappy. They often feel abandoned, cast aside, and uncared for. They may be frightened and just as often angry. Sometimes children scream and cry. They throw things. They hit other

---

[1]The term "parent" or "parents" is used in this book to denote the person who is the primary caregiver for a child, such as a mother, father, grandmother, aunt or uncle, older sibling, or foster parent.

The words "center" and "schools" are used to indicate a range of settings including infant and preschool day care centers, nursery schools for three- and four-year-olds as well as for toddlers and two-year-olds, and kindergartens.

children. They try to hit the teacher. They bite. They kick. They lie on the floor and have temper tantrums.

Sometimes the situation is very different. A child walks into the classroom as if she belongs there, as if she has been there a thousand times before. She handles the equipment. She plays with other children. She blithely waves good-bye to her parent. She speaks in a friendly way with the teacher. "What a great kid!" we say. "No problem at all. Just left her mother and got really involved in the program." Then one day, her mother leaves as usual and the girl collapses into a torrent of tears. No one can console her. She wants no part of any activity. Her behavior is completely unexpected. Her teachers feel bewildered and frustrated.

Other children may hide their feelings even more. They appear quiet and nonassertive. They seem to walk parallel to the life of the classroom. Often they are overlooked because they do not cause trouble. They seem self-sufficient and unassuming. A closer look may reveal that they are not involved with the materials of the program nor with other children to any significant degree. A teacher might think that such a child is mildly unhappy or has a low-key disposition.

Children who feel sad or troubled about leaving the person or persons to whom they are attached do not always make those feelings known to the teacher.

The parent may say he does not act that way at home. Such a child might be physically at school but psychologically at home.

Children frequently respond to the newness and the strangeness of an unfamiliar place. Some become agitated and race around the room, poking, prodding, touching, and looking. Others seem to be uncomfortable; they hang back and explore with their eyes while their bodies remain inert.

Not every child who comes into a classroom is affected in these adverse ways. Some march in full of confidence and behave as if they naturally belong in the room. For them the first day of school may be the culmination of a summer of anticipation or the reality of a longed-for adventure, shared originally, perhaps, with an older sibling. Some may be quite used to school or group care through prior experiences, although this may have the opposite effect for certain children who did not work through their separation feelings the first time around. Others seem to enjoy the novelty of the situation, the excitement of being with other children their own age, and the pleasure of new playthings. However, most children react vigorously in some way to new surroundings, though that reaction may go undetected. It seems that children do mental and emotional work to absorb and understand a novel setting.

Children need to size up the human environment as well as the physical environment when they enter a new classroom. The teacher becomes an object of intense interest and curiosity. They wonder: Does the teacher speak my language? Is the teacher my color? Are any of the teacher's mannerisms or attitudes familiar? Are the teacher's reactions to my behavior like my parents' reactions?

Factors like these contribute to a child's sense of strangeness or comfortableness because young children tend to define the whole adult world in terms of the behavior of their own parents. Children often expect that all adults will behave as their parents do. For example, if mother leaves every morning in a rush to catch the bus and father cooks breakfast while singing, chances are that the young child believes that all mothers and fathers do that in the morning. If mother does not allow water play in the bathroom sink, the child may believe that all mothers prohibit this sort of play and might even be surprised at the mother or teacher who allows it. In sum, children come to school with a set of expectations about adults built on their experiences. It takes time and new experiences with a variety of adults to teach them that adults behave in many different ways.

Because they enter school with these preconceived notions about adults, children may be very uncomfortable as they begin to perceive that the teacher does not behave like their mother, father, or grand-mother. Perhaps the teacher says it is fine to play with water, or talk while you eat, or get your hands dirty with glue. Children need time to put this new category of adult into their working intellectual scheme. They need time to differentiate between what goes on at home and what goes on at school. They need time to learn about the teacher, to learn what certain tones of voice mean, and to learn what to expect in various situations. They need time to sort out the differences between their teacher's and parents' behaviors. If the teacher is a benign and caring person, a child who is ready for school or group

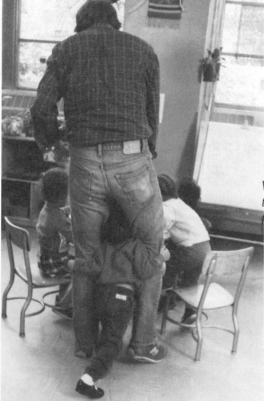

When a child trusts, she transfers her loving feelings from parents to teachers.

care will be able to transfer feelings of "basic trust" (Erikson, 1963) from home to school.

Until children come to feel this sense of trust, however, the teacher and the classroom remain strange. Day by day, familiarity replaces the unknown. This gradual process begins with the relationship between teacher and children. As children perceive the teacher in more trusting terms, they often begin to expand their relationships to the physical environment and to other children more openly. Establishing comfort with the teacher as a base enables children to become comfortable with the whole classroom.

Research has revealed a similar process in infants (Bell, 1970). Babies, it seems, first need to know that people are trustworthy and here to stay. They gradually learn that mother is not out of the world when she is out of sight. After that, babies are able to extend that concept to the physical objects in their world. It is by means of consistent, intimate human relationships that children become related to the larger physical and human world.

Children may feel strange in a new group that is unlike the familiar family group in which they have a special status. Few people know their names. No one knows whether they like vanilla ice cream or chocolate, or what frightens or comforts them. No one really likes or dislikes them in any particular way. They do not have a natural place in this group but will have to earn it, through their behavior. While they do not know this yet, perhaps they sense it.

Children may worry that no one will take care of them, that they will not know how to get home, that they will not be able to find their parents, or that their parents will not be able to find them. The younger the child, the more intense these feelings of fear. Some researchers conclude that until children are around three years old, they cannot retain a stable inner mental image of their absent parents (Mahler, Pine, & Bergman, 1975). Words or explanations of parental whereabouts are often ineffective with such young children until they trust the new adult.

The way children approach separation may also be determined by their particular family style. One family may be flamboyant; good-byes and other emotional events may be treated in a demonstrative fashion. Another family may be more reserved; their feelings are not openly revealed and meaningful events are handled with outward composure.

WHAT MIGHT PARENTS BE FEELING?

Sometimes teachers say that it is not the child who is having trouble separating but the parent. Surely a child's feelings are intimately bound up with those of his mother or father. Parents may have various kinds of emotions when they bring their children to school for the first time. It is not possible to understand a child's feelings without simultaneously acknowledging the parent's feelings. School entry is a significant event for both.

Parents may wonder: Can the teacher really take care of my child? Will the teacher understand him when he makes requests? Will the teacher like her? What will the teacher do if my child misbehaves? Will she humiliate me or enhance me in the eyes of the teacher? Will he reveal things about our family that are private? What will happen if my child gets hurt in school? Can I really trust this teacher with her? These nagging questions make it difficult for some parents to hand over their son or daughter to a teacher's care.

Parents may worry about how their children will get along without them or how they will function without parental control, guidance, or protection. In situations where parents have not left their children outside the home before, this feeling may be particularly strong. In some cases it may be less worrisome if this is a second or third child. Alternatively, a parent may expect the separation to go more smoothly with a second or third child and that may not be the case. However, more depends on a child's personality and relationship with the parents than the birth order.

One source of this worry may be the parents' ambivalence. On the one hand, they want their children to go to school or to group care. It gives them some much-needed time away from their children— time for themselves or time to pursue their work. Sometimes parents, normally, want to "get rid of" their children. They may secretly want to experience life as it was before they were parents. On the other hand, they love their children and wish to keep them near, to protect them, and to make sure all goes well with them. These ambivalent feelings are often uncomfortable for parents. When school begins, they may worry unduly about their children as a means of covering up, to themselves, their feelings of joy in their newfound freedom.

Parents may have other concerns as well. They may worry about the teacher's competence. The teacher is, after all, a stranger, and it

What might this parent be feeling as she bids good-bye to her daughter?

is not easy to leave one's child with a stranger. Why should a parent trust an unknown entity? Why should parents believe that a teacher will take as good care of their daughter or son as they would? Parents need some hard evidence that their children are in truly good hands to alleviate this worry.

Parents may also feel jealousy. "Suppose the teacher takes better care of Delores than I do?" "What if Eddie loves the teacher more?" Parents may find it hard to willingly entrust their children to a potentially conflict-ridden situation.

Parents may further be concerned that they, as good parents, will be unmasked. "Suppose the teacher finds out that Paolo is not really the great creative genius that I believe he is?" What if the teacher discovers the child's flaws—that she is a thumbsucker, he wets the bed, she kicks and bites, he uses fresh language, she is disobedient? "Will the teacher see me as a bad parent when she discovers these traits in my child?" Parents often feel that they will be judged by the teacher when they bring their child to school.

Some of these parental feelings are understandable when they are examined in the light of the parents' own histories. Parents themselves were once children in school. Perhaps they, like their own children, were shy or fearful about going to school for the first time. Parents also have feelings about teachers that are based on those past experiences. These feelings often resurface at school beginnings when parents recapture some of their own experiences with school entry and separation. Feelings of fear, anxiety, worry, and discomfort mixed with excitement are not unknown to parents as they enter a classroom with their children for the first time.

At a parents' meeting, a father said, "I felt good when George started in this center because he didn't have to worry about being late. When I started school, I always had to worry about being late. When I was late, the teacher got angry. Here they don't worry about 'late.'"

An Informal Survey of Parents' Feelings

I sent a questionnaire to a group of forty-four parents whose children, aged ten months to four years, were in three different day care centers. The parents were black, white, and Hispanic, male and female, and their socioeconomic status ranged from factory workers to college professors, from maintenance workers to doctors and lawyers. I asked them three questions:

What were your feelings when you knew that your child would soon be entering school or group care?

How did you feel the first day you accompanied your child to school or group care?

How did you feel about the separation from your child and your child's being in the teacher's care after the first few weeks had gone by?

Of the twenty-two who replied, many parents said they had mixed feelings when they knew their children would be entering group care. While they felt good because they knew, from friends or from experience, that the center was a safe and trustworthy place, they also felt worried about a variety of matters. Some worried about leaving their children. They wrote:

Was she too young at fourteen months? Would she become depressed or more clinging because of the separation?

My first feeling was that we were going to be apart for a couple of hours each day.

Sadness and loss that he was getting older and separating more from me.

How would she adapt being out of the closeness with me?

Some parents were concerned about their children's behavior:

Would she perform well?

I started thinking about how he would react when told to do something. How he would act when told to settle down the same time the other children do. My feelings are very deeply concerned with him being able to function correctly.

Some of the parents reported they were entirely positive about beginning group care for their children, but one commented, "Well, I wasn't happy because it was really the first time she would be away from me for a few hours a day, outside of her being with my family." In describing their feelings when they actually accompanied their children to school, parents used words such as "nervous," "anxious," "sad," "worried," "apprehensive," "tense," and "strange." All the parents, except one, admitted to these emotions. Two said they thought they felt more nervous than their children did. Several stated that they felt it was a "loss," a "milestone," "a big change that she was starting to grow away from me." Several expressed very strong feelings:

It was very hard for me to leave, and I had tears in my eyes.

I also missed my child a lot. I felt anxious about what would happen in the new surroundings.

I didn't feel too good because I wasn't used to leaving my daughter with people I really didn't know.

Others expressed their worry about leaving a daughter or son with strangers. One parent wrote, "It's a little bit difficult for the parents because they are entrusting people they still don't know very well with what is most precious to them—their child."

Some parents made connections with their own experiences with separation. One wrote that she felt "Nervous. Excited. Apprehensive. Thrilled. It brought back fond memories of my first day of school— a day I had eagerly awaited for many months." Another felt "somewhat sad and tearful about leaving her this time and thinking about all the other partings in the future—and past, I'll bet."

One parent of a twenty-month-old recalled the third day:

[It] was probably the most traumatic for us both. I left the school after dropping him off. He cried miserably. I went home to clean the house in a torrent of tears and guilt for being a part of a society that uproots babies from their mothers at such a young age. That afternoon, when I picked him up, he was listening intently to a story. We both cried and embraced after a long separation.

After the first few weeks had gone by, all the parents said they felt better. They used words such as "wonderful," "confident," "relieved," "secure," "positive," "comfortable," and "fine." These positive feelings built up because the separation was gradual and they saw that their children were happy. "She liked it, so I felt wonderful because the teachers treated her fine and she was happy with the other kids." "Yet in time," another wrote, "I learned that she just enjoyed it here very much. The teachers were supportive and wonderful to me as well as my child." Another summed up many of the other parents' feelings when she wrote, "As soon as a child shows signs of happiness, one feels relieved."

Trust in the staff seemed to be at the core of parents' resolution of their anxious feelings:

I felt that he was in good hands.

I felt much better than I had anticipated. This was just another step but nothing anxious or worrisome. I trusted the staff.

Several parents wrote about the support toward growth. "I still enjoy our times together," one parent said, "reading, playing, and experiencing new things, but we are both happier being able to grow in our separate ways."

Just because parents feel less worried after the separation has been tested and tried does not seem to mean that the initial feelings disappear entirely. One parent wrote, touchingly:

I still wonder if I've made the right choice. There are times during the day when I miss her very much. But it is a great comfort to me that she is so near where I work and I can readily go to see her and that she is in the care of such a wonderful staff. I think I would come to visit even more often, but the thought of coming and then leaving again sometimes deters me. As you can see, I'm not very good at partings.

Starting school clearly arouses many feelings in parents.

WHAT MIGHT TEACHERS BE FEELING?

You may be among those who feel tremendously confident when school begins. You may feel excited at the prospect of meeting a new group of children, or you might feel nervous about the first days. Perhaps you worry about what to do with possible criers. You might have concern about how long their crying will last. Perhaps you feel uncomfortable being around many parents for several days. You may experience feelings of anger at some parents who seem to be "pushy" or others who seem to be uncaring. Having parents in the room for any length of time may be unpleasant. You may wish to get them out as soon as possible. Perhaps you do not look forward to the first few days because of the strain and emotional drain it causes. Once the routines are established and children are comfortable, you may breathe a sigh of relief and feel that finally you can get down to the business of teaching.

There is nothing unusual about teachers feeling some of the same worries and discomforts that children and their parents are experiencing. Just as parents were once children in school, so were teachers. They have memories of their own school beginnings, some of which were positive and some probably not. These memories contribute to

Sometimes it is a strain on the teacher to control her own emotions when a child is protesting his parents' departure.

the feelings that are aroused as you become involved in first-day activities.

You may also have had personal experiences with several other forms of separation, such as graduation, vacations, changing jobs, moving, divorce, marriage, or death. How you were affected by any of these situations in the past may influence how you feel and behave in the classroom when school begins.

Other feelings, especially those related to parents, may be a source of difficulty. You might be eager to have them leave the room, even before the children are ready to let them go. You may find yourself at odds with some parents and in conflict with them about what is best for a child. Dealings with parents often arouse in teachers feelings they have, or had, about their own parents.

A group of teachers participating in a workshop on separation was asked to think of a word they associated with the word "separation." Here are some of their responses:

Fear
Anxiety
Pain
Alone
Angry
Venturing forth
Out of control
Rejection
Help
Distance
Unhappy

For almost all, "separation" conjured up a collection of feelings that were raw and unsettling. When discussing their responses they explored the reasons for such unhappy associations. Their personal experiences with separation seemed to be the most potent molder of their present feelings—how their parents treated them when there was a separation. "I was told to be a big girl and not to cry. I was probably only four or five years old," one participant recalled.

They also saw past stressful events, such as the birth of a sibling or their own parents' absence from home for an extended period of time, as influences on their present feelings.

Some found that striking out on their own and venturing forth were gratifying separation experiences that led to intellectual expansion and new levels of self-confidence.

Perhaps if you examine your own feelings when school begins or when a new child enters your center for the first time a connection to some of the emotions described here will be revealed. Once you are able to understand some of your own feelings, you may be more alert to similar feelings in parents and children.

The Impact of Separation Is Complex

Separation affects children. It affects parents. It arouses feelings in teachers. School beginnings can be exciting as well as uncomfortable occasions. Along with those who are genuinely delighted to be starting school, there are frequently crying children or tense and nervous parents. Often teachers feel pulled by the conflicting needs of the children, the demands of the parents, and their own inclinations.

Where shall I put her sweater?

Could I have a few words with you privately about Melissa? She's a very sensitive child.

Where will the bus leave him off?

Please don't let her drink grape juice. It stains her clothes.

Mommy. I want my mommy. Where's my mommy?

By the end of the first day, your head may be spinning from the accumulated problems and concerns of the children and parents, mixed with the excitement of a new group and a new year ahead. A situation that provokes so many feelings and so many memories is bound to produce reactions in all who are involved.

2

The Meaning of Separation

No fear arousing situation is missed or camouflaged as often as is fear that an attachment figure will be inaccessible or unresponsive. (Bowlby, 1973, p. 200)

Separation is an experience that occurs in all phases of human life. It starts at birth when the infant leaves the known, nine-month inner home for the strange outer world of bright lights, sounds, and the touch of human skin. It is seen in the wobbling of toddlers, practicing separation as they scoot away from a beckoning parent. Preschoolers experience separation as they leave the security of the home to enter an unknown world of the school. School-age children mourn the loss of friends who move away. Separation characterizes many events in developing adult life—an adolescent breaks up with a girlfriend or boyfriend; a young adult graduates from college and charts a new course; adults move to a new home; a person changes jobs; someone gets married, another gets divorced; a spouse dies.

All these events are bound by a common thread. In each circumstance, an individual is leaving familiar territory and entering the unknown, the untried. A potential for growth and change exists in every separation experience even though a temporary sense of loss predominates. Few people set out on a new venture without thoughts of what they have left behind.

Sometimes ceremony lessens the impact of a loss by acknowledging a particular separation as a legitimate transition to a new phase of development. In some primitive cultures rituals such as shaving a child's head may symbolize cutting him off from his past connections and indicate his entry into another stage of life. Spanking at a birthday party may be a modern counterpart of this custom. Other present-day events such as debutante balls, graduations, baptisms, bar and bat mitzvahs, and weddings mark the transition from one stage of life to another.

School beginning is also a transition to a new stage for children as well as parents, but there is no unique ritual that is culturally shared. A new lunch box, a pair of new shoes, a pencil case, or a new jacket or cap may be symbols to mark an event that is full of meaning and possibilities for children, parents, and teachers. Yet they share no tradition to ease them through this important occasion.

ATTACHMENT: THE ROOTS OF SEPARATION FEELINGS

Many young children display strong reactions when they are separated, or even anticipate separation, from their parents. Where do the roots of these feelings lie?

There is some speculation that the roots are very deep. Two pediatricians, Marshall Klaus and John Kennell (1976), postulated the existence of a sensitive period immediately after birth in which babies and their parents were predisposed to bonding.[1] Their research prompted them to conclude that this bonding was essential for parent-child attachment and had far-reaching consequences. While these findings have aroused controversy (Lamb, 1982, Lamb & Hwang, 1982), and qualification by Klaus and Kennell (1982) themselves, the idea that early and extended parent-infant contact is important has influenced hospitals to change maternity practices in an effort to be more humane. Whether or not early and extended contact affects the quality of attachment remains to be seen, but the fact that more parents and their newborns are permitted to remain together to strengthen the attachment process is noteworthy.

Though it may be an influential factor in development, this early bonding phenomenon is qualitatively different from the stable, deep, and abiding attachment between parents and children that is usually formed during the first year of life. This evolving attachment continues

---

[1]"Bonding" refers to the parent's feelings of concern and commitment toward the newborn infant, while "attachment" describes the enduring emotional tie between child and parent growing out of their day-to-day interactions.

to be magnetic throughout the whole of life and has been defined as a tie that binds one person to another in space and endures over time (Ainsworth, Bell, & Stayton, 1974). Often this attachment prompts a parent to rush to the bedside of a sick child, though the "child" be an adult, the parent elderly, and the distance many miles.

The term "attachment" has special meaning. It is not the same as "dependence." Although the two terms are often used interchangeably, they are significantly different. Children who are securely attached to their parents have an abiding trust in their parents' reliability, which fosters their own burgeoning self-reliance and self-confidence (Ainsworth, Bell, & Stayton, 1974). Children who are dependent sidestep their own thrusts toward autonomy and lean on their parents instead. According to John Bowlby (1969), the author of a major work about separation, dependence, which refers to an infant's state of helplessness, is present at its "maximum at birth and diminishes more or less steadily until maturity is reached, [whereas] attachment is altogether absent at birth and is not strongly in evidence until after an infant is past six months" (p. 228). He further describes dependency in human relations as a condition to be avoided and attachment as a condition to be cherished.

Many attachment relationships are characterized by trust.

Frequently, young children, who tightly hold their parents' body or hide in their clothing when entering an unfamiliar school setting, are regarded by teachers as dependent rather than as attached. However, such actions are legitimate, inborn attachment behaviors that keep infants and young children close to their parents. Clinging, crying, calling, or following are characteristic of all young humans and are explained by ethologists (those who study the connections between human and animal life) as remnants of an urgent, primitive, protective mechanism.

Attachment relationships are not only defined by clinging or crying. Many are embroidered with smiles and joyous exchanges when parents and children strike a comfortable balance with one another. These children seem to have an intuitive understanding and faith in their parents' predictability. They seem to know each other well and to trust one another's behavior.

HOW ATTACHMENT DEVELOPS

Although there are speculations that bonding may begin immediately after birth, a wide variety of experiences must occur between infants and their parents before attachment becomes secure.

A baby may "belong" to its parents in the parents' view, long before the parents truly "belong" to the baby. Margaret Mahler, who has done research about babies and their mothers, has evolved a theory about the development of young children's sense of self (Mahler, Pine, & Bergman, 1975). She believes that for the first two or three months babies experience parents as extensions of themselves, unable to completely distinguish the boundaries that exist between them. A young baby is described as believing that the nipple containing milk appears in her mouth by magic, called up by her own desires to relieve her hunger pangs. If an infant could talk she might say, "Oh, I'm so hungry. What I need is some milk. Ah, here's the nipple with milk. How powerful I am to make it come to me when I need it." Mahler defines this as babies' sense of their own omnipotence.

Her theory states that at around four or five months of age a "hatching" takes place as babies begin to break out of the psychological shell that wrapped them and their parents together. Little by little they begin to perceive the difference between themselves and their parents and to know the parents' bodies as different from their own, the parents' faces as different from other faces. They begin to know and to prefer the parents.

Usually, by the middle of the first year, through intimate looking, touching, hearing, speaking, seeing, and by means of babies' own development, they have become attached to their parents (Schaffer & Emerson, 1964). They come to know that the parents are their own particular persons whose looks, smell, touch, and sound are special. This attachment is a basis of human relatedness from which children derive the capacity for strong feelings about important people. It is this that enables children to become friends and lovers, as well as enemies.

As infants grow and develop, their attachment to their parents becomes more complex, more laden with feelings and meanings for all involved. Evidence of the strength of this bond is seen at around eight or nine months of age when babies often recoil, hide their faces, or sometimes shriek at the sight of a strange or unknown person. It is as if the baby were saying to the stranger, "I really know the person whom I love best—and it's not you." This occurrence is often called "stranger anxiety." As a child continues to develop, aided by the secure, certain relationship of his parents, this intense reaction to strangers usually begins to fade.

In fact, toddlers between ten and fifteen or sixteen months of age tend to be the very opposite of the suspicious seven- to nine-month-olds. They are like joyous world explorers, especially in the company of their parents. They have been described as having a "love affair with the world" (Greenacre, 1957). When not in the company of their parents, toddlers of this age often seem in low-key moods. They seem to be most free to explore when they have a secure base from which to roam. Mahler refers to toddlers of this age as "practicing" (Mahler, Pine, & Bergman, 1975). In practicing their newly acquired walking skills, they behave, and often look like, drunks. They freely wander off to see new and thrilling sights that have opened up to them, now that they are upright.

With this tremendous new scope to their lives also comes a particular danger, according to Mahler's theory. Their separateness from their parents is now a physical reality. They realize that they are vulnerable, that they still need care and protection. This realization often drives them back to the arms, laps, or legs of their parents for "emotional refueling" (Mahler, Pine, & Bergman, 1975). It is often bewildering to the parents and to the caregivers of toddlers between eighteen and twenty-two or twenty-four months of age that such formerly "independent" beings could become so clingy. This period, which Mahler calls the "rapprochement crisis," is frequently one of the most difficult periods for both parents and teachers (Resch, 1975; Rodriguez & Hignett, 1981), because, as Resch puts it, "all hell breaks loose" when children are left in group care or even at home with babysitters.

Not only are most children this age painfully aware of their need for their attachment person, but they are still developing the cognitive, as well as the emotional, ability to deal with that person's absence. While many children are able to call up in their mind's eye a mental image of that person by the time they are eighteen or twenty months old, that ability is not always reliable. This internal picture develops out of the pleasurable, as well as the not so pleasurable experiences that the baby has, from birth on, with the prime caregiver. The stability of that image is highly influenced by the toddler's emotions. Under tense, stressful conditions the mental image is often harder to maintain than in relaxed, comfortable times. For toddlers, out of sight is often out of mind. It is very hard to bear. It may seem to these young children that the beloved, missed adult will never return. Prolonged crying, intense rage, and uncontrollable sobbing are common in eighteen- to twenty-four-month-old toddlers. It is not surprising that parents and teachers often feel incompetent, frustrated, or even frequently angry at children in these circumstances.

When a toddler becomes a two-year-old, the intensity of these attachment feelings continues to be aroused when separation occurs or is even suspected by a child. For a child of twenty to twenty-four or twenty-six months, separation can be especially difficult. By this age, children have attached significance and strong feelings to the departure of parents, and they often become inconsolable at separation, even those of short duration (Resch, 1975). Two-year-old children have a profound understanding of the importance of these special parent persons. They know, deeply, their own tremendous need and reliance on them. This knowledge increases their terror and panic when that person leaves them.

Translated into the language of a child, those feelings might be stated like this:

I really know that you are my parent. I know that I need you to take care of me in all situations. I am afraid that if you leave me, I won't be able to take care of myself. It makes me angry that you want to go away like that, and I feel sad and hurt. So, in order not to feel that way, I'm going to do what I know how to do best to keep you here. I can cry. I can hold on to you, I can follow you, I can call you. These things ought to work, because they've worked before.

That is what attachment has been described to mean to very young children.

ABOUT SEPARATING

As children grow into preschoolers of three and four, separation reactions take a different form from those they had at age two. For one thing, most children have completed the phase of their "second" or "psychological" birth (Mahler, Pine, & Bergman, 1975). They have emerged from infancy and toddlerhood with a clearer sense of themselves as individuals, attached to, but distinctly separate from, their parents. They are described as having attained a state of "constancy," which is "the enduring inner conviction of being me and nobody else" (Kaplan, 1978, p. 35).

Another reason that three- and four-year-olds may handle separation differently from two-year-olds and toddlers is that they are able to consistently mentally represent their absent parents. As any adult knows, there is some comfort in being able to conjure up in your thoughts the person you are missing. Out of sight is no longer out of mind.

Being able to separate, becoming a "real school person" at three, four, and five is most gratifying and pleasurable for many young children. Often preschoolers are excited by the new environment replete with attractive playthings and a bevy of children their own age. Separation for these children is an adventure and a challenge. Eventually the ability to separate is a necessity if children are to develop as autonomous and self-reliant beings. It is a capacity that teachers applaud and most parents try to support. It is built up in preschool children through the cumulative separation experiences they have had, such as staying with friends, grandparents, and sitters, and going to birthday parties or to visit in other children's homes.

However, the ability to tolerate the stress of separation and the ability to adjust to strange and new situations vary greatly from child to child. Not all three-, four-, or even five-year-olds are able to enter school with complete comfort.

Certain developmental abilities are needed. They have been cited by Anna Freud (1965) as necessary to a preschooler's competent entry to nursery school. She states that self-feeding and control of bowel and bladder are prerequisites because they indicate growing bodily independence. The ability to relate to other children and to accept them as partners in their own right, plus the ability to use play materials in self-initiated and directed activities are further indications that young children are ready to enter nursery school. Freud also states that impulse control and the ability, at some times, to wait a turn, tolerate frustration, and express negative feelings appropriately are also necessary to insure a child's successful entry into school.

We all know many children who, on entering school, fit these guidelines and are able to leave their parents with a minimum of stress. We also know other children who do not entirely fit these descriptions and for whom entry and continued presence in the nursery school or day care center is stressful and unsuccessful.

Since parents are largely the mediators of their young children's experiences, they help children understand the meaning of events and other people's behavior in the way they explain these to children and the way they, the parents, behave. Parents translate separation at school in many different ways and communicate a variety of ideas and feelings about the event to their children. Often these ideas and feelings are expressed through the attachment relationship, so it is not very easy for a teacher to distinguish a secure attachment relationship from one that is insecure.

Here at school entry lies a ripe opportunity for teaching. Self-confidence arises from separations that are well achieved. Children who are supported by their teachers and parents as they separate from home have the opportunity to move fearlessly into new realms of learning and growth.

3

Learning from Children's Behavior

Children communicate with us through their eyes, the quality of their voices, their body postures, their gestures, their mannerisms, their smiles, their jumping up and down, their listlessness. They show us, by the way they do things as well as by what they do, what is going on inside them. When we have come to see children's behavior through the eyes of its meaning to them, from inside out, we shall be well on our way to understanding them. (Cohen & Stern, with Balaban, 1983, p. 5)

What are some of the clues children give us about their feelings connected with leaving home and entering school? Often "leaving home" is a more powerful experience than "entering school." Separation events usually involve a slipping back or a giving up in order to step forward. When learning to walk, children eventually give up crawling. When graduating from high school, adolescents give up the security of known teachers and friends to go forth to college or into the work world. When leaving nursery school for kindergarten, children leave a familiar setting. There is little growth without some pain or anxiety. As we step forward to a new level or challenge, we necessarily leave something behind. Without these dips and rises life would be flat, and people would be undeveloped. Yet the younger the individual, the more help he or she needs in moving forward without wounds. Children tell us through their behavior that they need our help, that their feelings are too overwhelming to manage alone. Let us look at some of these behaviors to become aware of their possible meanings.

VERY GOOD BEHAVIOR

Sometimes children are very good in school. No one can tell they are hurting inside. They keep to themselves. They never get into trouble. Teachers often overlook them in the midst of the swirling life of the classroom. Such a child was Kelly.

Kelly was a four-year-old boy. His face often wore a blank expression. He rarely smiled. He never cried. He spoke very little. When the group had a music and singing time, Kelly stood at the edge of the seated group, watching. When the group sat for juice and crackers, Kelly sat, but refused to eat. When his mother brought him to school, and when she came to pick him up, he was compliant and obedient. He never made a fuss.

Kelly hardly played with any of the equipment. If he painted, it was a lackadaisical three or four strokes of the brush and he was done. He

What may be some of the reasons that a child sits at the edge of an activity?

seldom spoke to other children and only spoke to the teacher when asked a direct question. He spoke in short phrases or single words.

When, by November, Kelly's behavior had not changed, the teacher became concerned. She had one clue. Since this was a cooperative nursery school, mothers periodically helped in the room. When Kelly's mother came to help, the teacher noticed a dramatic difference in Kelly's behavior. He was talkative, he ate lustily, he used the equipment, and seemed to get pleasure in his play.

The teacher arranged a conference with the mother to discuss her concern for the vast difference in Kelly's behavior with and without his mother. They came to the conclusion that perhaps Kelly was missing his mother. It seemed to the teacher that while Kelly was physically in school, he remained mentally at home.

Together, they made plans as if Kelly were again starting school from the first day. His mother began to stay in the room with him for about one hour each day. They talked about his missing her. They played together. They planned for her to stay each day that week until snack time. After that first week Kelly and his mother decided together that she would stay once a week. She did so for a month.

At the same time his mother was in the room, Kelly began to relate to the assistant teacher, staying close to her, speaking softly to her. She discovered that if she sat next to him at snack time, he would wait until all the children had left the table and then would eat. He still refused to participate in music time, so the assistant sat next to him, while he stood watching the group. She read to him, led him to the table, and encouraged him to play with dough while she sat next to him. He began to talk more, to both children and adults. He began to use the play equipment. His body relaxed and his face began to exhibit more variety of expressions. By March he had begun to eat when the others ate. By April he began to make a friend and after spring vacation, he sat near the music group. One day, with the assistant's hand holding his, he took a turn walking around in a circle to the music, wearing his cowboy hat.

He had finally come to school.

It was fortunate that Kelly's teacher recognized his lack of involvement in school activities as a separation reaction, even though it was November. By allowing him the time he needed to coalesce his home self with his school self, his teacher helped him to grow in competence and in self-confidence.

It was also an advantage that his mother was a nurse and that her working hours permitted her to be with Kelly when he came to school in the morning. Another parent, with more conventional working hours, might have been able to stay at the end of the school day, or arrange to come for lunch. Perhaps phoning at strategic times might have helped.

Sometimes, however, children are not at all ready to enter school or group life. If, for example, Kelly had not made a relationship first with the assistant teacher and then with the children, if he had not started to play, if his body and facial expressions had not relaxed, if he had not started to eat, then he might have been telling his teacher that he was not ready to leave home, not ready to come to school. While such situations do not happen frequently, they do occur. Teachers need to be aware of such a possibility and to think about such questions as

How will you help parents understand that their child is not a failure? How will you help a child understand this?

How will you keep in touch with the family and make it possible for the child to try again?

What will you do to alleviate the anxieties of other children in the group who might worry that they, too, might not be ready?

What will you say to the other parents who might ask, "What happened to that boy? Why isn't he here anymore?

DELAYED REACTION

Often children do not send out the strong cues that Kelly did. They may come to school bright and bouncy, delighted to be there, excited to play, full of fun and pleasure.

Three-year-old Tania cheerfully kissed her mother good-bye every morning. She painted with enthusiasm, used many colors, and seemed to enjoy her activity. She used dough and water with pleasure and found companionship in the dress-up area. She loved music and books and puzzles. She was a happy-go-lucky girl.

One day, three weeks after school began, she threw herself on the floor, crying hysterically for her mother. She was inconsolable. The teacher phoned her mother that evening to ask if anything unusual had happened. The mother could think of nothing. After all, she recalled, the move to this present new home had taken place several months before.

After that, Tania cried repeatedly when her mother brought her to the center. Together the teacher and the mother decided to see if it would help if the mother stayed a little longer each morning rather than leaving right away. It took several months of this maternal support before Tania felt safe. Even so, Tania occasionally cried for her mother and refused to play.

The move to the new home seemed to be a bigger event in the life of this small girl than anyone had realized. It had taken many months for the child to internalize that experience. It was not until she had been in the center for a few weeks that she was able to express her great distress. Two separations, one from her old home and one from her mother, were more than she could bear.

Children do not have the experience with loss that adults have. They do not know that there are boundaries to these experiences. Children often feel that the loss will never end, that they will never stop feeling sad, that they will never stop crying. They need help to understand that life is not all like this and that the lonely, sad times have ends as well as beginnings. Tania's teacher and her mother, working together toward a common goal—Tania's comfort and ability to control her life—helped her to grow toward the belief that she was a strong person who could overcome hard-to-bear feelings. Tania also learned that though these feelings continued to overwhelm her at times, she could count on her teacher to comfort and support her.

REGRESSIVE BEHAVIORS:
THUMB SUCKING, EATING, WETTING, SLEEPING

Tania regressed in her behavior, slipping back to a stage of development that was reminiscent of the toddler. Rex Speers, a psychoanalyst, found that children entering nursery school normally repeat phases of their earlier development (Speers, McFarland, Arnaud, & Curry, 1971). He believes that this repetition is desirable for children's successful adaptation to school. As they behave in ways that echo their past, Speers says, children make use of their mothers' presence in the classroom to gain self-assurance. Such normal regressions occur when children cry, complain, plead to be taken home, refuse to play, and cling to their mothers tenaciously.

Sometimes children need to fall back a few steps in order to then

In entering nursery school, children may interact with their parents as they did when they were toddlers.

move ahead. Perhaps you have noticed that tendency in yourself or in other adults. I once knew a writer who, before she could sit down to the serious business of writing, spent half an hour sharpening every pencil in the house. It was a bit of regressive behavior that seemed to provide the needed energy for the task before her.

One of the most obvious remnants of much younger behavior in preschoolers is thumb sucking. Some children who had given it up may, with the onset of school or day care, begin again, only to give it up once more after they become comfortable. Others who still need to suck their thumbs might be seen sucking more frequently, especially when their parent leaves, at transition times, or when they eat or sleep. It is not uncommon to see children increase their thumb sucking at the end of the day, when they are tired. Some children might also want to return to the comfort of a bottle, even though they had stopped using one. They might need to bring their bottles to school to use for comfort in times of stress.

Do you feel uncomfortable seeing these behaviors in your classroom? Do you know why? You may worry that if one child has a bottle, or sucks her thumb, that all the children will want bottles or their thumbs. Parents may share these concerns. It is highly unlikely that this will occur, however. Children behave in certain ways because of some specific need. If other children do "copy" them, they will only do it for a short time unless they, too, have a similar need.

Can you observe a child and decide what it means to him to suck his thumb or bottle? Is it important to him? Does it comfort him? Does he engage in other activities in the room besides sucking? When does he stop sucking? How can you provide him with more of the times when he does not suck?

You may notice that when he is engaged in activities such as water play, clay, painting, or blocks, he is not inclined to rely on his thumb. A cooking experience or a collage project may offer him worthy substitutes for the self-stimulation of his thumb. In general, children feel better when they are productive.

Another regressive behavior related to sucking is seen in eating. The three-year-old in the following anecdote becomes troubled about his snack.

> Although Sean was busy with blocks, he noticed the teacher handling grapes for snack. He stood up quickly, dropping the block, and cried softly as he rushed over to the teacher saying, "No, I don't want this, I only want crackers for snack." He spoke quickly, with much feeling.
>
> "Come and look at the food, Sean," said the teacher gently. "These are grapes, and this is cheese. You don't have to eat them, but just come closer and look."
>
> "I don't have to eat them," he whimpered.

Children often display feelings of stress at snack or lunch time. They may eat too little or too much. Food is frequently a tangible reminder of home, and you may see young children act in a worried manner about eating.

Regression is sometimes seen in children's physical movements. In a study by Curry and Tittnich (1972), children who were "graceful and skillful in performing motor feats" at school entry "suddenly [became] quite clumsy, tripping over nothing at all and causing all sorts of accidents to [themselves] and others" (p. 13).

> Ellie was swaggering in large circles around the room attending to the children and their activity rather than where she was walking. She focused on the children to the front, side, or back but not on those directly next to her. As a result she tripped and fell three times over children and toys

Enjoyment of eating is often a good clue to comfort.

that were in her path. As she fell, she glanced at the obstacle, then immediately regained her far-sighted vision. Her movements were quick as she
scrambled to her feet, arms straight, with the palms of her hands flat on
the floor to balance herself, as a toddler might.

Toilet accidents and sleep disturbances, especially among two-and-
a-half- and three-year-olds and sometimes even among four- and five-
year-olds, are generally common in stressful situations. These regressions of well-learned skills frequently happen around the time children begin school. Parents may complain of bed wetting, constipation,
stomachaches, or wet underpants and clothing. Children may resist
going to sleep at school as well as at home. Nap or rest time may
find children fidgety, squirming, tense, or unable to stop talking or
giggling. Parents may report children waking in the middle of the

night, having nightmares, or refusing to go to bed. The opposite may also occur—children who never napped begin to need one, or regular nappers take very long, extended two- or three-hour naps.

How many adults, faced with a trip across the country or abroad, moving to a new home, going to college, or starting a new job, find themselves plagued with constipation, diarrhea, loss of appetite, over-eating, or sleeplessness? Our bodies often express our feelings, even if we are not aware of them. Children and adults are much alike in this regard.

> Nicholas, twenty-six months old, took a daily afternoon nap at home. When he started day care, he refused to sleep. No amount of rocking, back rubbing, singing, or vocal soothing would induce him to sleep. Finally the caregiver stopped trying to give him a nap and allowed him to play after lunch instead. Often he fell asleep on a soft chair or couch. After a few weeks of this he allowed the caregiver to put him on a cot in the nap room.

Why might young children be so worried about sleeping at school or day care? In falling asleep, children give up whatever small amount of control they have over themselves when they are awake. Giving it up, for some children, is not easily done. It is especially difficult at a time when they are worried about where their parents are and whether or not their parents will know where to find them. Some children think that if they are not sure where their parents are, then their parents may not be sure where they, their children, are.

While regressions in motor control, eating, toileting, sleeping, and sucking are frequently associated with separation reactions, they are also commonly seen whenever children feel stress, either at home or at school.

LOOKING AND TALKING

Often children show through looking and talking that they are not yet able to rely on a mental image of their parent as a source of comfort and reassurance. They require an extra dose of teacher and parental help.

The parent can be seen sitting nearby. The distance between parent and child is distinct yet minimal, fostering the boy's developing capacity for trust.

Two-and-a-half-year-old Christopher needed his grandmother to sit in the room with him for more than a week before she was able to move to a small library room connected to the classroom. Christopher often walked into the room and circled around her. When he was in the classroom, he frequently looked in through the open door, checking to see if she were still there.

A child's internal picture comes from repeated interactions and experiences with the loved person. The ability to hold this image develops slowly and in toddlers is unstable when the person is away. Christopher used his eyes as well as language as techniques to maintain his grandmother's image.

"I will not cry," he said. "No, I will not cry. Nana will not go? No, Nana will not go. She will be in the library. She will not leave Christopher. Christopher will go to school. Nana will wait in the library."

Despite the grandmother's repeated reassurances that she would wait in the library, he asked the same questions again and again.

Children's use of language may provide other clues to their feelings about separation. Refusal to talk, reversion to baby talk, or excessive talking may be signals that a child is worried.

> Four-year-old Shawnique never spoke a word to the teacher during the entire year. She spoke only occasionally to other children although she played frequently with them. She used materials, listened to stories, and sat on the teacher's lap but she refused to speak to her despite the teacher's most creative efforts. Her mother said that she never stopped talking at home.

This girl's refusal to speak possibly indicated her incomplete separation adaptation. Perhaps it was her way of leaving a part of herself at home.

While some children may display anxiety through silence or continual talking, others may use language to master their feelings. Teacher's words, too, can help, even with the youngest children. However, "Mom will be back as soon as we've had lunch" is reassuring only if it is true.

Sometimes children use words to reassure themselves, as if the words themselves had a physical presence.

> Every morning, Miriam looked at her mother and questioned, "Are you going to work? At the hospital?" "Yes," her mother replied while kissing and hugging her. "Bye bye! Have a nice time today."
>
> Miriam took the teacher's proffered hand, saying, "My mommy is going to work. To the hospital. I'll stay in school. She'll come back to get me, right?" The teacher reassured her that her mother would be back after work. Miriam went to paint at the easel.

Through their language children have the ability to let you know that they need help.

> Arthur, in the midst of snack time, begins to sob. "I want my mommy!" Three other children watch him intently. The teacher hugs him and says, "I guess you're missing your mommy. She'll be coming back soon." He stops crying and reorganizes himself. The other children seem visibly relieved.

Children's language offers other opportunities for a teacher to take some appropriate action. In a music session reported in a teacher's log, children share their feelings with the teacher, who is later able to sing songs about mothers and encourage children to move to music, permitting them to dramatize their feelings of missing their mothers.

> As we were about to start music, Demian buried his face in his hands and burst into tears. "I miss my mom!" he cried bitterly. I noticed several other children start to cry. Their faces seemed to say the same thing: "I miss my mom!"
>
> This was not unprecedented. We had been having a rash of children missing their mothers over the past few weeks, but nothing as blatant as this. For this reason, I had made a family scrapbook. Children had brought in pictures of their families and could look at them in times of need.
>
> When I asked the children if they missed their moms, they all, with definite feeling, said they did. As I began playing a soft song, everyone with the sole exception of Norman, got up and started dancing. The children moved gracefully, feelingly to the music. There was a sharing of this "I miss you" emotion. Norman sat on the sidelines, observing wistfully. (Small, 1983, p. 31)

Coping with separation may take the form of using baby talk instead of more mature language. You can help children by acknowledging this regression as a normal step in growing up. Admonishing them to speak in their normal manner often makes them feel ashamed for having shared their secret longings with you. In the following anecdote, the teacher who used music responds to baby talk in his four-year-old group.

> As the group settles down for music, I noticed Eleanor and Amy engaged in "Ga Ga" talk. I saw a dazzling array of different feelings expressed through playful body language and cooing tones. I had the feeling that they were completely themselves. Vanished for the moment were the pretenses and obfuscations of feelings so often accompanying the use of proper language.
>
> Sensing the moment ripe for baby movement, I asked, "Show me how you move like a baby." Silence. Shocked, blank faces. The children momentarily became stupefied when confronted with the reality of acting out some of their repressed fantasies.
>
> Finally, after a long silence, Adam volunteered. He is strong, secure, and playfully rebellious—far removed from a helpless "baby self." He was in a position to venture into the "baby" role and have fun with it.
>
> And what fun he had! Getting on hands and knees, he playfully crawled,

rolled, and scampered around the floor. All the while he made playful, realistic baby sounds. Soon all the others followed. (Small, 1983, p. 25)

INCREASED DEPENDENCE

Perhaps you have seen otherwise competent children become increasingly dependent during the first weeks of school or day care. They refuse to dress themselves or protest that they cannot, demand help in the simplest of tasks, refuse to pour their own juice or milk, need your lap many times during the day, and cling, follow, or shadow you or other adults in the room. These behaviors seem to say, "I am feeling very little and not up to my usual competent self. Give me just a little extra babying for a short period of time and it will provide the fuel I need so that I can get up and go on my own steam."

Parents may report to you that they see similar behaviors at home. Les wants to be dressed in the morning; Jason refuses to be dressed. Camillo constantly crawls into his mother's lap; Annie follows her mother from room to room, crying if she goes out of view. You will begin to know that these are beginning-school behaviors. They are, for the most part, temporary and will probably disappear as the children are reassured that their parents have sent them to school or day care to have a good, happy time and that the teachers can take care of them. Trust of this sort takes time to develop.

Have you ever noticed that many behaviors associated with eating, sleeping, competence, language, and toileting are exhibited again by children when they return to school after an illness or an extended absence? Have you noticed children behaving in some of these ways when strangers enter the room for a visit? Or when the familiar room arrangement is changed? There seem to be common elements in these situations.

SECURITY OBJECTS

Remember Linus and his blanket in the *Peanuts* cartoon? We laugh at Linus because we have so many children in our classes who bring shreds of blankets, tattered and rubbed-out stuffed animals, old diapers, or other "cozys" to school with them. Perhaps you remember

Where she goes, there goes her blanket.

A stuffed animal helps when a child is feeling lonely. Sometimes it is hard to put down even when there are attractive activities.

having such a security object yourself. Somehow these things seem to make children feel good, as though they have brought a bit of home with them to school.

Children seem to grant security objects special qualities and endow them with important powers. Just watch what happens when a boy or girl misplaces his object and cannot find it! A well-known psychiatrist, D. W. Winnicott (1957) calls these "transitional objects." He explains: "It is not the object itself, of course, that is transitional; it represents the infant's transition from a state of being merged with the mother to a state of being in relation to the mother as something outside and separate" (p. 183).

The teddy bear or blanket supports children's journey to growing up from infancy to early childhood. This journey leads them away from being part of the parent toward being persons separate from the parent. Because these objects have such significance for young children, they seem to provide a sense of security when children move from the familiarity of the home to the unfamiliarity of the school or center. The objects children bring from home are often more important than the activities to which they are drawn in school:

> Illana worked with pegs and puzzles while holding on to a ring that was far too large for her to wear on her finger. She would not let go of it even though it made using the manipulative toys she was working with more difficult. (Paul, 1975, p. 40)

Sometimes children use things from the classroom itself as transitional objects in an effort to master their separation feelings.

> Daniella strode over to the dress-up shelf. She began to throw clothes and shoes haphazardly over her shoulder, tossing them into the air, until she found her favorite black derby hat. She popped it on her head. A large grin immediately appeared on her face.
>
> Several times during the day she was seen looking at herself in the mirror while wearing the derby. For months she frequently wore it all morning, even putting it under her cot when she took a nap.

Since children also turn to their security objects during transitions in the day's schedule or at times when the curriculum breaks down, you will need to distinguish between those situations, heightened other stress, and separation reactions.

RELATIONS WITH OTHER CHILDREN

Through their uncomfortable relations with other children and with adults, young children often show that separation is more stressful than they can handle. This may take the form of belligerence or withdrawal. Do not assume that all angry behavior is connected to separation reactions, however.

The same Christopher who worried and clung to his grandmother in the library also provoked others and disobeyed the teacher.

Christopher saw a plastic cauliflower that Joshua had dropped on the floor. When Christopher grabbed it, Joshua, astonished, said, "Hey, that's mine!" Angrily, Christopher threw it in Joshua's face. Joshua yelled, "I don't like that!" and glared at Christopher who opened his eyes wide, laughed mischievously, and ran off in circles all around the room.

When the teacher told Christopher to pick up the cauliflower and to talk to Joshua about it, Christopher ran to the bookshelf and sat down to look at a book.

Why would children who are feeling worried about separation hit others, be disobedient, or destroy things in the classroom? Consider this: One way to get rid of scary feelings is to fight them by taking very active steps. Throwing things, hitting, or arguing with others gives one the illusion of tremendous activity. It is as if children feel that they must do something to make themselves feel less worried. They are less concerned with the consequences of their antisocial behavior than they are with eliminating the fear they feel.

Sometimes children behave in a frantic manner:

Adam . . . flitted around from one thing to another. . . . When the teacher tried to get him to [complete] a drawing, he told her . . . "I can't—you do it!" He treated the guinea pig like an inanimate object . . . he ran around the room as if he expected to be chased.

He did not pay any attention to his mother . . . when she left. But when a girl spoke to her father on the play phone, he grabbed the phone out of her hand and said, "When are you coming back?" On a number of occasions he ran in the opposite direction when he was told that it was time to go home and that his mother was waiting for him.

Although he seemed almost desperate to make contact with children, he went about it by repeating what they said, grabbing things from them, taking over what they were doing, and trying to create excitement by getting silly with them. (Paul, 1975, pp. 36–37)

COPING THROUGH PLAY

It is, perhaps, through play that children find their most satisfactory means of coming to terms with and mastering their reactions to separation. Developing cognitive skills is necessary for children to understand separation (Resch, 1975). Before age three, a child begins to attach meaning and feelings to a parent's departure. To the extent that he can use a caregiver's presence and eventually language and play to find relief from sad and angry feelings, he shows his potential for growth.

> Three-year-old Marina throws her doll out of her room every morning before going to school. She tells her mother, "I don't want to go to school." Her mother acknowledges this by saying, " I know you don't want to go." Then she helps Marina dress, gives her breakfast, and takes her to school. Marina initiates a hide-and-seek game with the teacher when she arrives. This goes on for several months.

What can we say about Marina? Is this a problem or is this a child at work, coping with leaving home and going to school? Marina is using symbolic play to aid her adjustment to this new experience. She is practicing control over her own life. It is she who throws the doll out of the room, unlike the real situation in which she is taken to school. In playing hide-and-seek, it is she who has the control, unlike the real situation. In the real situation she has no control, for it is her mother who decides to take her, and leaves her at school.

As adults, we attempt to manage our feelings and behavior when events occur over which we have little control. It is when we lose control, when we are unable to rally ourselves to take action, that we feel unsatisfied with ourselves and defeated. Children feel the same way.

Role playing is an important and self-initiated activity that serves a multitude of functions. Through roles, children try out various ways of "being." Taking on the role of the one who offers nurturing may be one way a child can be both nurtured as well as nurturing. In tending to a doll, a girl may be caring for the doll as if the doll were herself. In the following anecdote of two three-year-old boys, the roles of baby and mother are clearly enacted, allowing both children to feel cared for as well as caring.

The child feels nurtured as well as nurturing.

Andrew is the mother. At his feet is a wicker laundry basket with Nathan sitting in it. He is the baby. Andrew gives Nathan an affectionate look and asks, "Do you want more?" The "baby" replies in a high, squeaky voice, "Yes." Andrew carefully places himself down into the basket, half resting on the edge. His chest is about on eye level with the "baby." He sticks his chest out, offering his "breast" to the "baby." The "baby" pretends to suck through Andrew's shirt. Andrew wraps his left arm snuggly around the "baby's" neck. He has a very serious look on his face.

Play of this sort may help children feel more confident about their parents' continuing nurturance even though they are not present. Witnessing such an intimate scene may cause some adults discomfort. However, it is natural for very young boys to "try out" feminine, as well as masculine, activities in their play.

Make-believe is a rich resource of healing for preschool children. You may see children soothing their own feelings as you observe them at play. You may see them attempting to gain control, as in "fighting fires."

Gerald was riding a trike and making siren-like sounds. He abruptly jumped off the trike and ran toward the opposite end of the playground, yelling, "Fire! Fire! Quick, there's a fire over there. Get the fire hats, hurry!" He pulled a hat out of the box, plopped it on his head, and rushed back toward his parked trike, shouting "Hurry! The fire! We need to put out the fire! C'mon! Fire! Fire!"

Perhaps the dangerous fire was a symbol for things that often raged out of control in Gerald's small life. Play is one way a child can practice being in charge.

As children begin to adapt to school and to the temporary loss of a parent, they begin to demonstrate their tolerance for "the existence of 'goodness' or 'badness' in [themselves] as well as in [their] mother" (Curry & Tittnich, 1972, p. 28). They play out this theme in different ways. It may involve "good baby–bad baby" games, "good guy–bad guy" roles, or, as in the following anecdote, a girl's being "bad" herself.

Jessica rushed over to Jamie, quickly grabbed the car from his hand, darted across the room, and hid behind the teacher. When she saw Jamie rushing toward her, yelling "Jamie's car!" Jessica dropped the car and ambled over to the telephone. Picking up the receiver, she shouted, "Bad girl! You are a bad girl! Bad girl! You are such a bad girl!"

This play helped Jessica, who was having difficulty leaving her mother, come to terms with the good as well as the bad in herself. A month after this incident, she became a full-fledged class participant. Though the "bad" behavior resurfaced, it was short-lived. Her entry into school was both positive and enthusiastic.

Jessica swooped into the room, ran over to Jamie, and snatched a small car from his hand. When Jamie protested loudly "No!" and half-rose to his feet, Jessica dropped the car, ran over to her cubby, skillfully unzipped her coat, and hung it on the hook. She rushed over to the shelf, picked up a toy car, plopped down next to Jamie, and pushed her car next to his.

The younger the children the less able they are to use fully developed play in their attempts to gain mastery over their feelings. Children two and under are more directly imitative than symbolic in their play, yet this form of play gives them a chance to express themselves.

Rebecca, nineteen months old, had spent most of the day in the center in a happy frame of mind.

> After lunch several children arrived at the center with their parents for the afternoon session. As one after the other of the parents bid good-bye to the children, Rebecca began to cry. She stood near the door, sobbing, repeatedly waving "bye-bye" and throwing kisses.

In reenacting the morning parting from her own parents Rebecca gave vent to feelings that she had been containing. Her expression of such deep emotion drew the caregiver to her, and she accepted the comfort of a lap and a hug.

Play can also take the form of interacting with materials such as blocks, paints, crayons, water, or dough. Through the creation of something with these materials, children are able to externalize some of their worry about separation. For example, three-year-olds often fear masks. They frequently believe that a mask is real and that the person wearing it is, indeed, a wolf, monster, or witch. They are equally afraid of putting on a mask. Perhaps they believe that if they do, they will change identity or that they will disappear. They may believe, when they see a teacher put on a mask, that she has disappeared and has now become the witch or wolf. Here there are similarities with separation. The younger a girl or boy, the less able they are to understand that when a person leaves, he or she does not disappear. So it is with masks. While most four-year-olds understand that a teacher still exists beneath the mask, many three- and two-year-olds are just as sure that she does not. Thus, for a three-year-old, making a mask and being in charge of putting it on and taking it off in front of a mirror may be one way of adding some understanding about the appearance-disappearance aspects of separation.

> Isaac came close to the paper bag masks that the children were making. He seemed frightened and started to run away. He watched intently as the teacher put on a mask. When he looked through the holes in the bag and saw the teacher's face, he laughed. He placed a paper bag over his own head and looked at himself in the mirror. He began to select materials to paste on the bag. He became relaxed and thoughtful. Finished, he sang out, "I made a mask!" patting his chest for emphasis. As another teacher walked by, Isaac shouted with glee, "I made this. I'm gonna scare you!"

Children use the theme of appearance-disappearance in a variety of ways. Peek-a-boo is an age-old favorite that children begin to play as early as six or seven months of age. In those early months, the game allows the baby to experiment with the permanence of things and people. First you are here, then you are gone, and now you are back again! It is a way of learning that things and people exist even though they are not in sight. Babies play it again and again; learning that there is stability in the world takes a long time.

This game also allows young children to develop the means for coping with separation. In essence, separation is, after all, "You're here, you're gone, and now you're back." Peek-a-boo is both a rehearsal for and a recapitulation of the separation experience.

There are many variations on the theme of peek-a-boo. A two-year-old who wraps and unwraps his play dough with a large sheet of paper is playing the game in his own style. The following anecdote reveals how Jamal, a two-and-a-half-year-old who had a hard time separating from her mother, plays out some of her feelings with a small covered box containing a toy bear and a tiny blanket.

> Jamal cried hard for a long time after her mother left. When she finally calmed down, her eyes lit on a small box. She opened it and grinned when she saw the bear inside. Removing the bear and the tiny blanket, she laid them both on the floor. Then she put the bear back in the box. "He's crying," she said, as she patted him. The box fell over and the bear rolled out. "Do you want to go to sleep in there?" Putting the bear back in, she said, "I cover him up." She closed the box and carried it as she walked around. Again she put it on the floor, opened it, and took the bear out. Rubbing her fingers over the bear, she put him back in and closed the cover. Opening the cover, she patted the bear three times and said, "G'night."

In comforting the crying bear, Jamal seemed to be reenacting both the feelings she had when she cried as well as the comforting she received from her teacher. In the ritual of opening and closing the box, taking the bear in and out, she may have been reassuring herself that her mother, though gone, would come back. A significant aspect of this play situation is that the child has the upper hand. It is the child who says good-bye, who does the leaving, who controls the appearance and disappearance. This sort of play adds to a child's growing sense of self-reliance.

WHEN PARENTS RETURN

We have been focusing our attention on children when they are left by their parents. However, we must not neglect the reunion of parents and children at the end of the class session or at the end of the day. What happens then is often revealing and frequently misunderstood.

Have you ever had an experience like this? A parent comes to call for her son, expecting a warm and loving greeting at the end of the school day. No such thing happens! The boy refuses to leave, runs around the room, begins to paint or takes blocks off the shelf, tries to put on dress-up clothes, or insists that the teachers now need his help in cleaning up the room. The parent begins to become annoyed and is forced to insist that the boy come home. He goes reluctantly.

On the other hand, a child may cry when a parent comes, may refuse to speak, or may turn away from parental attempts at a hug or kiss.

What could be operating here? You might think that the child likes school better than home or the teacher more than the parent. While that may be true at some moments, it is not true in the majority of cases.

All during the day, children have been actively managing their angry or sad feelings about being left. When the end of the day comes, they find it hard to maintain that coping stance, and they may break down. Crying shows that they have reached their limit of dealing with these feelings. Refusal to go home, giving a parent a hard time, and acting as if they do not wish to greet parents in a loving way are all behaviors that say, in effect, "You left me here this morning. Now it's my chance to leave you by staying here. Now I can give you a dose of what you gave me this morning."

While in most cases, a child's avoidance of parents at reunion time is normal, there are some cases in which you may want to take a closer look. If a child consistently ignores or rejects his or her parents, in the mornings as well as the evenings, this may indicate a problem in the parent-child relationship. A small percentage of the children in the studies done by Ainsworth (Ainsworth & Wittig, 1969) refused to respond to their mothers at reunion, ignored them, or rejected their attempts at greeting. Because of the persistence of this phenomenon, she labeled such children as ambivalent in their feelings toward their mothers or as "insecurely attached." If you have concerns about a particular parent-child pair, you may want to consider having a conference with the parents. If you feel that the problem is beyond your competence, you may need to seek help from a child guidance center or a child psychologist.

It is not unusual for teachers to interpret children's rejecting-of-parents behavior as an indication of their own superior ability to form a relationship with the child. This leads to competition with the parents, which is never helpful to child or parent.

OTHER SEPARATION REACTIONS

Separation reactions do not always go away after children have happily settled in the classroom. They may appear in a variety of other situations, and you may be surprised to see some of the old behaviors appearing in related situations. Perhaps you teach a group of four-year-olds. As children begin to have their fifth birthdays, you may notice an increased anxiety in some who begin to talk about kindergarten. Many four-year-olds believe that on the day they become five they will go to kindergarten. They begin to suffer the separation blues until they understand that they will not have to leave the security of their present school immediately.

Feelings about separation may erupt in situations that remind children of their original separation experience. A resurgence of clinginess or a renewal of crying may occur when children return to school after an illness or a vacation. It is as though they were going through a shortened version of their first school entry. There may also be a revival of these reactions when the teacher returns to the classroom after having been away for a time. It is not unusual for children to express angry feelings toward their teacher for being away from the classroom for a few days, no matter the reason for the absence. You may also be aware of these reactions on Mondays when children leave home after the weekend or on Fridays when children leave school or group care.

Your reaction to children will be important. Accepting these feelings with understanding aids a child's knowledge that certain emotions are appropriate. Such understanding will also help parents who may be mystified by their children's behavior in these circumstances.

Similar reactions are frequently seen at the end of the school term.

Children are not very ceremonious about saying good-bye at that time. Many teachers feel let down when children blithely skip out the door without so much as a backward glance. One teacher I know found herself in tears as the last child nonchalantly left the room. Often young children cannot comprehend that they will not be coming back the following week.

Some children do feel the pain of parting on the final day but do not know how to express it. The following record of a child's last day is a good example of the mixed feelings of anger and sadness that many of us, children and adults, feel when an important event draws to a close.

> At the final day family picnic, Janine passes by the two teachers who are seated on a blanket. She shoots a quick glance at them and runs to her father.
>
> She returns in a few minutes with a ball and starts to play—still not too close. Although the teachers speak to her, she does not look at them. When they ask her to sit with them, she gives them a hostile stare.
>
> Abruptly, she runs across the grass to a table where slices of watermelon are available. Gazing wistfully at her teachers from that distance, she eats her watermelon. Slowly she approaches, again appearing nonchalant, pointedly not responding to their remarks. She refuses to join them on their blanket, but sits on the grass, her back to them. Suddenly, she turns and says, over her shoulder, "Hey, I'm scrapin' this watermelon like an artichoke!" Showing the teachers the rind, she scrapes it with her teeth. Then, just as suddenly, her face becomes downcast and she crawls up between the two teachers and, touching both, curls up and puts her thumb in her mouth.

HOW YOUR OBSERVATIONS CAN HELP

Your own keen observations of children's behavior are a most fruitful source of knowledge. Taking brief anecdotal records of the child and parent on their first day, or during the first week, may provide a rich resource for both helping the child and conferring with a parent if the need arises. Be alert to the possibility of your own bias warping the actual observed behavior. There is a world of difference between the two following brief anecdotes of the same incident. In which one does the teacher's bias come through?

> Cindy sat in her mother's lap during the entire morning session. Her body was rigid and she frequently covered her eyes with her hands. Her mother cradled Cindy in her arms. She made no attempt to interest Cindy in any of the activities.

> Cindy is a really spoiled child. Her mother is no help at all, holding Cindy close to her on her lap. Cindy doesn't even try to play with anything.

It is not unusual for teachers' opinions or expectations of how children should behave to interfere with their "seeing" what is happening. Taking records of children as they arrive with their parents, as well as when they leave with their parents, may provide a close-up of the separation process. If such records are taken over a two-month period, at two- or three-week intervals, you may be able to identify patterns of separation for individual children. Observing and recording behavior associated with separation will increase your awareness and aid in your daily planning for those whose separation is not smooth.[1]

Becoming aware of the ways in which young children communicate their concerns about leaving their parents puts you in a firm position to help them. Coping with stress and gaining mastery over feelings are important requisites for maturing. Assuming that children will "get over it" or "grow out of it" does not provide them with the opportunity to work through their feelings. In an environment of understanding and support, children become competent and self-confident. They learn not only how to leave, but how to venture out— how to try new things.

When you say, "Sure you can sit on my lap. I know how you feel. You must be missing your mom," you are helping a girl or boy understand that their feelings of loneliness and grief are both legitimate and acceptable. You are helping them cope with those feelings through your friendship. You are helping them understand that their feelings have an end as well as a beginning. You are helping them master their feelings by putting those feelings into words. You are helping them know that you have confidence that they are persons who can cope with those feelings, can receive help from another human being, and can then go on to act in an age-appropriate way with pleasure.

---

[1] One source of information on taking anecdotal records is in Cohen and Stern, with Balaban (1983).

You are the person who can do the most for children when they enter your classroom for the first time. Your support and caring helps children grow toward independence.

They are on their way, with your help, to becoming sturdy, happy preschoolers able to function successfully without their parents in a safe, nurturing, and trustful environment. It is you, the teacher, who has provided them with this possibility for growth and with the potential for coping successfully with many future separations (Furman, 1972).

4

Your Role: Using Curriculum

Children need to learn that adults can be teaching, loving, and helping people. Teachers show children this through daily actions, courtesies, and gestures that do not detract from children's feelings of competence. Such actions by adults will help children want to grow up like the caring adults around them. (Honig, 1982, p. 20)

In chapter 3 we looked at behaviors that provide clues to children's feelings as they begin school or group care. We also considered some ways that children cope with their fears and tensions about separation.

What can you do to encourage children's attempts at coping so that they emerge from their school separation experiences as strong, capable, and self-reliant individuals? How can you use your curriculum to fortify these children?

Curriculum begins with you, the teacher. It is based on what you know about the developmental abilities and needs of each child in your class. Curriculum for young children is what happens between you and the children, between the children themselves, and between the children and the activities, events, and materials you have chosen to provide. Curriculum is not merely a series of lesson plans or "recipes" that tell you how to do what in each situation that arises in the classroom life.

Water play, for example, cannot be described as effective curriculum apart from you, the teacher. As curriculum it depends on how you set it up, how you understand its value, how you mediate between the children and the uses they make of the water, and what your reasons are for offering it to the children. If you stand near the water play area, mopping up every spill, admonishing children to be careful, or directing children in how to use it, you are providing one kind of curriculum. If you allow the children to explore the water freely in their own ways, perhaps covering the table with toweling to minimize spills and encouraging them to clean up themselves, you are providing a very different kind of curriculum, certainly a different experience for the children.

The topic of separation is as viable an aspect of early childhood curriculum as water play. Similar thinking applies. The use you make of separation as curriculum will depend on what you believe about separation and how you choose to use it in the day-to-day life of your classroom.

Think of separation as a curriculum process rather than as a single event. Imagine curriculum as a necklace with several strands of beads. One of those strands is called "separation." It stretches from the beginning of the school year to the end and is dotted with beads representing different activities. However, no one bead alone makes up the strand, as no one strand makes up the necklace. As you begin to provide children with activities to alleviate their separation stress, you will be providing them with your knowledge of the psychological roots of attachment and separation, and your ongoing concern for their positive growth and development. You and the children are the strand upon which the beads are strung.

Let us, at this point, reexamine the characteristics of separating children described in chapter 3 in order to reflect on curriculum decisions.

CHILDREN WHO ARE "TOO GOOD"

The important first step is to decide that you want to help "too good" children. They are often hard to reach because they demand so much time and energy. You have to keep working at your relationship with them. This is admittedly troublesome because there is a class full of children clamoring for you. These quiet "good" children do not always make speedy progress, and it may take many weeks of reassurance and your continuing attention until they are able to function on their own. It may also necessitate parent contact, which is described in chapter 5.

These children often need interchanges with you alone before they

Young children often need a trusting relationship with an adult before they can explore relationships with other children or with activities.

are able to relate to other children. Stories read while the child sits on your lap, games played with you, and clean-up chores done together are opportunities for intimate contact that build a trusting relationship.

The following excerpts from a teacher's two-month observational log give a close view of her work with one of these "good" children.

> *11/10*   Diana seems to love the affectionate attention of other children, but she is not yet ready to interact with them. She does not seem to have a strong voice of her own yet. Her sparse language, her tentative steps may indicate that Diana does not feel entirely comfortable about classroom life.

> *11/13*   Diana still seems not quite in school. She has a faraway expression and roams around, touching a puzzle, a book, but can't seem to settle anywhere. "Would you like to do something with me?" I ask. She looks pleased and shakes her head "yes." We choose a stacking toy. She climbs on my lap, nuzzles into my arms, leans against me, puts her hand on my knees and I hear her breathe deeply.

11/20   Diana is using puppets, singing a song that comes from deep inside her, "La la la la." They are a very useful prop to get Diana out of her withdrawn state. She is really able to show a wide range of feelings, and the puppets have helped her get on with her language development.

It also seems as if the verbal interaction and the affectionate demonstration with momma and baby puppet helped Diana to deal with her separation feelings. She brought momma into the classroom when she needed her. A giant step for Diana.

11/26   Diana was very engrossed using crayons and paper. "Look," she said, "I made a girl." It was indeed a representation. The first she had done in school.

Later she began to tie her shoe. After much effort and concentration, she got the two loops together. Excitedly she flew over to me, "I tied my shoes myself!"

The two incidents, so close to each other, are further proof of Diana's growth.

12/11   I thought it would help finalize their separation if Diana could see her mom get on the elevator each morning and watch the door close. This kind of sequencing seems to help Diana. It gave her a certain amount of control over the separation, rather than *being* merely left.

12/15   Today is Monday—sometimes hard to say good-bye. When Diana came back from walking her mom to the elevator, she wore that old faraway look. "You have that look that says you weren't ready to say good-bye to mommy." She smiled a half smile. "Sometimes mommies have to say good-bye too soon and you have to say good-bye too fast." Diana grasped my hand. It must have felt good to be understood.

Later in the day, Diana was constructing a body of clay. "I made a girl . . . arms, legs, eyes, nose, and a tushie." She said it with awe. I had the feeling that now Diana had a greater sense of herself as a separate person. She has all these separate parts. This was an important observation of her.

12/18   Both my assistant and I feel that she is more ready to be in school now. She has begun to move away from adults and play with children.

12/19   Diana is really blooming these days. She seems to experience herself as a separate person. I feel that since I started this log she has been gaining strength. The log has helped me focus on Diana and give her more of the support she needs.

Through this log we see Diana emerging from her silence and her "good" exterior, becoming a person related to others and more comfortable with herself. Her growth occurred because her teacher fully believed that separation was a significant part of the curriculum for this child. The teacher's use of her own interactions with Diana, her empathy with how Diana was feeling, her one-to-one reading of books, her use of puppets, and her attention to the ritual of good-bye were all concrete actions that formed curriculum. This log illustrates that curriculum for young children is what is planned, what is thought, and what happens.

Have you any such "good" children in your class? Did you ever think that part of them, in a sense, never came to school—that part of them stayed home? Can you devise ways through your relationship with such children to test out this theory?

Perhaps your own diary of observed events in the school life of such a child would help you focus on the child's progress and on your role.

DELAYED REACTION:
CHILDREN WHO ARE "FINE," THEN FALL APART

How does the curriculum serve children who seem "fine" the first few days or weeks and then fall apart? What can you do? Some of the same things that strengthened Diana are appropriate—reading to them, holding their hands during transition times when they may be feeling lost, holding them on your lap when they seem low, sitting close to them at eating times, talking with them often, singing with them, or playing with them frequently.

You may fear that attention to one child will jeopardize your relationship with the other children. On the contrary, the others will feel reassured when they see you ministering to one child's needs. It is when a distressed child is not appropriately attended that other children become anxious and worried. Not that they will not have jealous feelings, but they will also feel that you can take care of them, too, if they are feeling unhappy.

Suppose you do all these things and none works. A child is still upset, crying, without joy or pleasure in your classroom. This may signal that perhaps he or she needs the added boost of a parent's presence in the classroom again. If the parents are free to come back, they may be of two minds. One is that they are willing to help their children in any way that seems reasonable, as Kelly's mother was able to do. The other may be that the children must "get over it" and that if the parents come back, it will only make the problem worse. Perhaps you believe that, too.

In the case where a parent's return makes the situation worse, it may be that the child is not ready for a school or group experience at all. In such a case it might be better to suggest delaying the start of school for a few months. What is truly difficult in such a situation is helping the parent and the child, and possibly yourself, to recognize that none of you has "failed." Adults often have definite ideas that equate "growing up" with "school." It is very hard to accept the inability to go to school in any terms other than failure. However, there is no such thing as failure in school entry. There may be only a slipping back, which requires help.

If a parent is working fulltime and cannot return to the classroom, more creative measures may be required. The teacher will be dramatically thrust into the role of a surrogate parent and may even find that the child's difficulties are a source of great emotional drain.

Actions that may help the child whose parents are unable to be with him are arranging phone calls from the parent to the child; keeping available a favorite object from home, something belonging to the parent, or photographs of the family; visiting the child's home; holding additional parent-teacher conversations and conferences; and/ or finding out what the child's favorite home activities are and doing them in school. Sometimes the teacher's support of a parent who plans to talk to her or his employer about the need for a bit of time off could be very important.

CHILDREN WHO REGRESS IN THEIR BEHAVIOR

At school beginning it is common to see children thumb sucking, having toilet accidents, talking very little or too much, not eating at all or overeating, becoming clumsy, clinging to a special object, refusing to nap, becoming aggressive, showing a lack of self-confidence, or being unable to play.

What are some special techniques that are useful for giving children comfort during the first few weeks of school? How can curriculum support children's regressive behavior and help them move toward self-confidence? Many of the suggestions made in connection with children who are too good and those who display a delayed reaction also apply to those whose behavior has regressed. No matter what kinds of signals a child sends out, your encouraging their expressions of feeling, through both words and actions, is the most significant contribution you can make to their growth. In the words of one expert, "The child who really copes well allows himself to miss the absent loved one, to feel sad, lonely and perhaps angry, and to express his feelings appropriately" (Furman, 1974, p. 16).

CHILDREN WITH PARTICULAR NEEDS

Children have a variety of needs stemming from particular circumstances. For example, some children come from single-parent homes, from homes with recently separated parents, from homes where there has been a death or chronic or serious illness of a loved person or pet. Some children's parents are depressed, retarded, mentally ill, or adolescents. Some children are disabled, mentally or physically. Any such circumstance may influence the quality of the parent-child separation. Teachers need to be especially sensitive to these children and parents. While it is true that their differences should be minimized rather than exaggerated, children may require special attention as they separate.

In a program for mildly retarded children, for example, it was noted that the children did not give the same kinds of clues to their feelings about separation as nonretarded children (Kessler, Ablon, & Smith, 1969). Their regressive behavior was often attributed to the retardation itself and the children's aimless running around to hyperactivity. As the teachers helped the mothers recognize their children's feelings of anxiety about separation, the mothers began to understand the depth of their children's attachment. The teachers also made special efforts to identify a child to himself by "showing him his own photograph, saying his name and verbally calling attention to what he was doing" (Kessler, Ablon, & Smith, 1969, p. 6). Then they attempted to develop in the child the same awareness of "mother." They talked about "where she is now, what she is doing, and the reunion with her" (p. 7). The teachers continually encouraged the expected, normal response to separation on the part of the children and in so doing enlisted the mothers' cooperation. Concretizing the separation process and a child's identity helped these children since they lacked conceptualizing skills.

ACTIVITIES THAT HELP
CHILDREN COPE WITH SEPARATION

There are many ways you can help children express their feelings about separation and cope with their emotions.

Specific Teacher Behaviors

Encourage children to participate fully in saying good-bye. Hugging, kissing, crying, waving, and saying "I'll miss you" are all ways of bringing feelings out into the open. Once in the open, they are easier to deal with. Never allow a parent to sneak out.

Talk with children about their feelings. This enables them to take verbal steps toward mastery of their emotions and control of their actions (Katan, 1961).

Help parents and children plan together for the next day's parting. Through such planning children gain security and experience self-confidence.

Provide an opportunity for children to watch the parent leave. Perhaps there is a window in the classroom through which children can peer. Steps placed by a high window allow children to look into the street as parents leave the building.

Regard all the "baby ways" that may appear, from thumb sucking to wet pants, without a fuss. The less attention you pay to such behaviors, even if you do not like them, the sooner they will disappear.

Be aware of transition times in your daily schedule, such as clean-up periods or moving from one activity to another. Sometimes those "in-between times" are especially difficult for children who are coping with separation. They may go out of control, hit other children, withdraw, suck their thumbs, or masturbate. Try to involve a child in activity right away.

Encourage children to bring a favorite toy or blanket to school each day, or something belonging to their parents. Allow them not to share these "security" objects. To the children, they are a bit of home.

Wall Displays

A list of children's names on a kindergarten wall chart will attract the attention of children and their parents. What a sure message to children that the teacher really wants them! If the names are printed large, with a felt tip marker, children who are able to recognize their own names will feel pleased. Children who do not read will feel equally delighted when their parents point out their names.

A wall poster in a toddler room announcing the names of each child's family members, including pets, welcomes parents and children. It helps parents to know one another's names. Such a welcome eases the entry to the center by making a firm connection to home.

Letters

Write a letter to the parent from the child. This is meaningful to three-, four-, and five-year-olds. Setting down "Come back soon," "I miss you," or "I love you" in words on paper seems to be very reassuring. The letter can contain a drawing or the child's own "writing" and can be tucked away in the child's cubby to be shared, or not, when the parent comes back. It will be up to the child to decide.

Photographs

Photographs of children's families, including pets, posted in an accessible spot help young children remember that their families really do exist, even though they cannot be seen. If these photographs are covered with clear adhering plastic, they will withstand lots of loving attention. Be sure they are hung at children's eye level so that they can be seen easily.

A special book of photographs about life at home may help ease the transition from home to school and provide an opportunity for parent involvement. A child could take the book home each day and bring it back to school.

A picture of the family tucked into a child's lunch box brings a warm reminder of home.

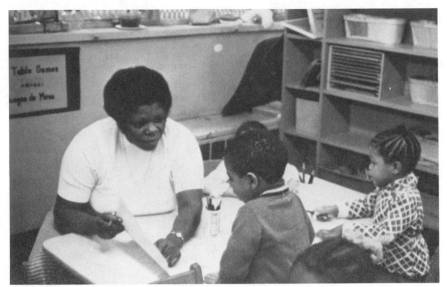

Juan has just said good-bye to his mother. The teacher is helping him write a letter to her: "Querida Mami, me haces falta. Regresa despues de mi siesta. [Dear Mommy, I miss you. Come back after my nap.]" After they finished, he took the letter to a private place and decorated it with special drawings.

How do cooking activities help children resolve their separation conflicts?

Cooking

Cooking activities link young children to home in a very concrete fashion. Nothing could be more familiar than food and its preparation, except its consumption. Cooking with children is a natural way to bring home and school together while at the same time creating opportunities for competent action and intellectual investigations. Shaping the cookies, mixing the batter, cutting vegetables for soup, or dipping bread into an egg-milk mixture for French toast are all activities that allow children to share the enticing world of adults. Here also are chances for mind stretching—reading recipes, calculating quantities, measuring, predicting outcomes (What will happen to the flour when we add the milk?), and engaging the senses.

Playing

Using puppets helps children express their feelings of longing for their parents. This is meaningful to preschoolers of three, four, and five. Children this age are attracted by animal puppets and often label them mommy, daddy, grandma, or baby. They will need you to help them by using your puppet to ask their puppets questions such as, "Do you go to school? Where is your mommy (daddy, grandma)? Do you have a baby puppet? Who takes care of your baby?" You may find yourself included in the play and perhaps assigned a role.

Games of peek-a-boo and games of hiding and retrieval can be played in sand and water where toys can be hidden and found easily. This is a way of practicing being left and being reunited. Such games give children control over the process of leaving and returning.

Provide for, and observe, children's natural dramatic play. This will give you consistent clues as to how children are doing in their attempts to cope with separation reactions. Children may play baby or nurturing parent many times over in their attempts to come to terms with their feelings. They may play themes of moving or going away. They may play monster as they begin to face their fears of being on their own in school. You can provide for this play by supplying props such as suitcases, dolls, a doll bed large enough for a child to lie in, and space and privacy for play. If you listen to and observe such play, you will find out just what means children use to cope with their feelings.

Playing baby in the doll bed is comforting. This child uses make-believe in her efforts to master her feelings.

Taking on a role enables children to experiment with another identity while strengthening their own.

Children make an impact on a blank piece of paper. It is a way of saying, "I am me—a separate, special person."

Satisfaction, a feeling of accomplishment, and a sense of competence come from the joyful involvement with nonstructured materials. How does this activity help children cope with separation?

Expressive Materials

Provide nonstructured materials such as paints, blocks, clay, crayons, felt tip markers, and clean drawing paper. This allows children to spontaneously represent their feelings about themselves, their families, and their entry into the new world of school. Some of those feelings may not be pleasant, and it will help if you are prepared to see both angry and sad feelings being displayed.

Books

Storybooks about how it feels to be separated from a loved one can open the way for children and adults to talk together about separation and to gain new insights into the process.

Choosing these books should be done with care. The first consideration is that the book be good literature. It should be pleasurable to read and pleasurable to hear. Does the book display clarity of writing style, brevity, interesting characters, and suitable illustrations? Is the story related to the child's own life experiences? Be certain that the book is free from stereotypes. It must also appeal to adults—it is very unsatisfying to read to children if the book is uninteresting to the reader.

Books that address sensitive topics like separation need other special qualities. In an article about the use of books in crisis situations, adults are urged to apply the following guidelines:

> "Can children identify with the plot, setting, dialogue, and characters? . . .
> Does the book use correct terminology, psychologically sound explanations, and portray events accurately? . . .
> Are the origins of emotional reactions revealed and inspected? . . .
> Does the book reflect an appreciation for individual differences? . . .
> Does the book present crises in an optimistic, surmountable fashion? . . . " (Jalongo, 1983, p. 32)

How you read the book to children is critical. First, be thoroughly familiar with the book before you read it to a child. Next, introduce it briefly by referring to a naturally occurring situation that may have prompted its use. Asking specific questions throughout, or after, the

Reading to a child alone, or in small intimate groups, gives children a close experience of being nurtured at a time when they may be feeling younger and in need of special care.

story "encourages children to analyze the behavior of the story characters, make inferences about emotional reactions, apply information to their own experience, and synthesize techniques for coping with crisis" (Jalongo, 1983, p. 34). Finally, summarize the story by rephrasing the basic story concepts. In this way, children's ideas and information can be clarified.

An annotated booklist for children can be found in appendix A at the end of the book.

Other Ways to Help

There are other ways you can help children achieve control of the separation process. Here are some suggestions:

If your school has a preschool opening "paint and get ready" spruce-up session in which parents contribute some working assistance, include children in some appropriate work. They can put the clean toys on the shelves, wash tables and chairs, help mount pictures, or label cubbies. This activity adds a measure of child control over the physical environment and affords them some familiarity with the room. Teachers, children, and parents can begin to know one another.

You can ask a child to tell you when his parent should leave the room. Shall it be now, or after snack?

When you take the group outdoors, you can ask a child to say good-bye to a parent who then stays in the room. This reverses the process, allowing the child, rather than the parent, to do the leaving.

During beginning days, children can choose the spot in the room for their parents to sit.

Once a child is secure in the classroom, you can encourage her capacity to separate through a variety of small separation experiences. For example, the teacher can ask the child to return a few lunch dishes to the kitchen, take a message to another teacher, or visit another classroom for a short period of time to hear a story or paint a picture.

Beginning Days

Beginning days and weeks are not the time for exciting trips or stimulating art projects. Children need time to get acquainted with the teachers and with the room and its materials. Careful planning for these beginning days is a necessity. There are many decisions to be made.

Do you want to put out all the blocks or just a limited number of shapes? Think about the age of the children and their former experience with blocks. Very young children of three and under may be overwhelmed by more than just three or four basic shapes in the beginning. On the other hand, kindergarteners, who may be experienced builders, might feel cheated if the block shelves were not full.

Will you start with several colors of paint or just one or two? Do you want to start with paint at all? Young toddlers may not be ready to use brushes and an easel in the early days of the program. They may need more time to control their small muscles, while older children may be ready right away to try their hands at painting.

Do you want to have hard as well as easy puzzles on the shelf? Are some of the children entering your group highly skilled in puzzles? You will need to think about children who may get discouraged if they try puzzles that are out of their range.

Will you provide paste with collage materials or will you wait until the children have been in the program for a while? Your decision may be based on the age and experience of the children as well as the amount of adult help you have in the room. If you have to spend a lot of time teaching children how to use paste, it may inhibit you from interacting with parents and children as freely as you wish.

Will you put out crayons or felt tip markers with paper, or both? Markers are very easy to use and respond best to a light touch. Think about the age of your children and the kind of touch they use. The younger the child, the heavier the touch. An eighteen-month-old does not have the finesse of a five-year-old.

These decisions will convey specific messages to children and their parents. A carefully arranged room with well-chosen materials in appropriate quantities reflects your serious attention to the needs of beginning days. When there is a certain order, a cheerful cleanliness, an array of attractive playthings that are not overwhelming, this will tell those entering your room that you have anticipated their arrival joyfully—and thoughtfully. Your pleasure, and your care, in their entry will prepare the way for a successful separation.

Social Life

The social life of a classroom is a slowly evolving, ever-changing phenomenon. Today's enemies are tomorrow's friends. "You can't come to my birthday" frequently turns into "Do you want to play good guys and bad guys?" Teachers play an important role in helping young children learn what it means to be a friend when they demonstrate friendliness, compassion, and respect for children. This model of an adult who is an enabler (Katz, 1974) provides the most meaningful lesson to the young. In an atmosphere of acceptance, children learn to be accepting; in an atmosphere of empathy, children learn to be empathic; in an atmosphere that encourages autonomy, children learn to be autonomous.

The understanding of social life develops as children's thinking abilities mature. In a study of friendship, children's ideas were shown

Making friends becomes possible when a trust of adults exists at a deep level. Only then is it safe to reach out to others and to commit oneself to the classroom world. Sometimes friendship takes unique forms.

to change as they became less egocentric[1] (Selman & Selman, 1979). Whereas in early childhood a friend is regarded as valuable because "she has a Star Wars toy," children develop, by early teens, an understanding of the reciprocal nature of friendship.

Helping children as they struggle to comprehend what it means to get along with others is a demanding task. It is often more helpful for the children to be asked "What happened?" in a conflict situation than for the teacher to decide who is at fault. Children need the opportunity to examine a situation and try to work out a solution with the teacher's help. They need as much chance to play alone as with others because social life requires that people be in harmony with themselves as a foundation to harmony with others.

---

[1]"Egocentric" is a term that describes young children's thinking. It is characterized by the assumption that the actions of people and events in the child's world are somehow magically connected to the child's self (ego). For example, a three-year-old eager to see snow asked, "If I take a nap, will it snow?" as though her napping could influence natural events.

Help young children define their separating selves by encouraging them to interact constructively with other children. By initiating and sustaining social interaction, you build a bridge connecting children securely to the human world. As these experiences for the children multiply throughout the school year, their trust in you and your program flourishes because it is built on a firm foundation.

ENCOURAGING CHILDREN'S COMPETENCE

Through a curriculum that has an understructure of support for separating children, teachers can provide many opportunities for them to develop and exercise competence. Helping them build self-confidence and self-reliance appropriately can make them feel comfortable and safe when away from the protection of their parents. The key word here is "appropriately." Even though two-year-olds, for example, might be able to do many things for themselves, it is not appropriate to assume that they never need holding or cuddling, or that they can solve interpersonal problems without the assistance of an adult.

The thrust to being capable, to making a difference in the world, to having an effect on the environment comes from within. It is said that such motivation is inborn (White, 1968). You who have been with children day after day know firsthand about their intense drive to do things for themselves. "I do it myself!" is a phrase familiar to every preschool teacher. It begins when children are under two years of age, with their actions saying what their words cannot.

Encouraging this innate motivation builds competence in the young. There are many opportunities in the preschool classroom for this: in carrying out the routines of the day, such as pouring juice, dressing, choosing foods to eat, or toileting; in selecting toys to play with or art materials to use and getting them from the shelves oneself; in taking risks, making friends, and choosing books. Achievement fills a child with pride and self-gratification. It is fed by the comfort and trust generated in a secure classroom environment. Separation is the "developmental necessity" underlying the child's discovery of himself as builder.

Your most valuable contribution to a child's development will be the recognition that separation reactions in young children are valid and expectable. Your own knowledge and your understanding of this

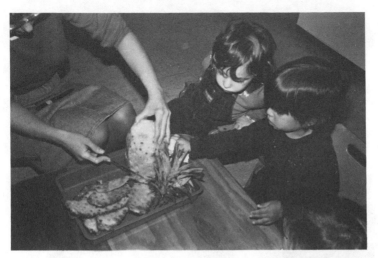

Competence is built in many ways in
the preschool environment. Through
trying new food,

through taking risks,
developing skills, and

through engaging with
books.

67

*A child discovers himself
as a builder.*

as a significant element of the early childhood curriculum will help children in your care to develop a strong sense of themselves as individuals able to feel sad, angry, and grieving. They will be able to develop the ability to cope with those feelings without being over-whelmed or rendered ineffective.

The steps children take in school to achieve this will help them practice the skills they will use in many different separation experiences all through their lives (E. Furman, 1974; R. Furman, 1972).

5

Parents and Teachers:
Learning Together

The developmental line of separation-individuation may be used not only in describing the developing relationship between a mother and her young child but in describing the relationship between parents and offspring across the entire life cycle. (Cohler & Geyer, 1982, p. 207)

Parents, children, and teachers are equal participants in the drama of separation and school entry. Each group has needs that require attention. This chapter addresses the needs of parents and teachers to learn from one another.

Every September newspapers carry stories about school openings that seem to verify the meaningful nature of this event. There are often photographs that dramatize the tension of starting school for children and parents. In the *New York Times* of September 14, 1982, Suzanne Daley wrote:

> The stuffed animal that goes everywhere with five-year-old Eric Benderisky went to Public School 9 yesterday. It was Eric's first day of school, and Puppy Dog's, too. Eric held one paw, and Eric's mother, Ruth, held the other, and that was the way they arrived at 100 West 84th Street. Eric said he was o.k. His mother said she was nervous.
>
> Elizabeth Sanchez kept her eyes on her son, Jason, 6, who had complained of a stomach ache before he left for school. "His older sister said some bad things to him about school, so he's scared," Mrs. Sanchez said.

Another school entry was described by Dena Kellman in the *New York Times* of September 9, 1980:

Diana Lambouras, who had taken her 5-year-old son, Emilio, to school for the first time yesterday, was standing in the rear of his classroom at P.S. 51. It was almost 2 p.m. and she had been standing there all day.

"I've tried to leave," Mrs. Lambouras explained. "But every time I do, he falls on the floor and starts screaming."

Mrs. Lambouras said she had asked her son this past weekend whether he wanted to go to school and when he had told her he did not, she said she had tried to change his mind.

"You'll learn to read and write, you'll make new friends," Mrs. Lambouras recalled saying. "You want to go to school, now don't you?"

" 'Yes,' " Mrs. Lambouras said her son had answered, " 'but you have to come with me.' "

Mrs. Lambouras agreed.

She said she planned to stay with Emilio today and even tomorrow. . . . "But next week," she added, "he's on his own."

Perhaps some form of preparation might have made this first day more comfortable, more predictable. A visit to the school by the mother and her son in the spring, a meeting with the teacher prior to the school's opening, mailing a written description of school beginning to the parents, and/or a parents' meeting held the week before school started might have contributed clarity and direction to the event. Perhaps a letter from the teacher to the boy would have been helpful. It is very exciting for young children to get mail. Perhaps a questionnaire for parents would contribute to the home-school relationship.

With children under three it is imperative that teachers' contact with parents be as ongoing, supportive, and close as it is with the children. When you think "children" of this age, you need also to think automatically "parents." There can be no distinction, for the way you treat the child affects the parents and the way you treat the parents affects the child. Your focus, as the caretaker/teacher of children under three, is the children themselves as well as their attachment relationship to their parents. While a greater distance has developed between preschool children of three, four, and five and their parents, they are, nevertheless, still bound very closely together. Respect for this bond is a major part of the school entry process.

Accepting this attitude will influence your manner of relating to parents. Every effort should be made for you and parents to have contact before the children arrive in your classroom. Parents need to see what sort of a person you are and how you work with children. They need to know some of your ideas about childrearing and to decide whether or not they agree with them. They need to feel that you are trustworthy and competent to take care of their dearest possessions.

"It's a little bit difficult for the parents," one parent wrote on a questionnaire, "because they are entrusting people they still don't know very well with what is most precious to them—their child."

In one center, parents are invited to observe the teacher in action with her present class before deciding whether to enroll their children. Such a preenrollment visit is actually the beginning of the separation process and is the first phase of the entry. The message to parents is (1) our center respects your judgment and your duty to know what kind of arrangements you are making for your child, and (2) we think our center is pretty wonderful and we want you to see it for yourself. Parents have every right to suspect that something is wrong with a center where no such visiting is allowed. This holds true for parents of three-, four-, and five-year-olds as well as the under-threes.

If the parents, after an initial visit, decide they want their children in your center, you will have your first opportunity to get to know them. Whether you arrange for a home visit or for a conference before a child's arrival depends on your preferences and the parents'.

Some parents find the idea of home visits nerve wracking. They may feel that they will be judged on the basis of how their living quarters look. Others may consider it an invasion of their privacy, while some families thoroughly enjoy the sociability of the occasion.

This first face-to-face contact is the second step in the entry and separation process. What might take place? What are some of the things you would want to find out about the children and their families? What are some of the things parents might wish to learn from you? Would you like the parents to fill out questionnaires to supplement your conference?

These conferences and/or home visits might be held during the first two or three weeks of school when some parents may still be in the classroom with their preschool children.

Mrs. K. arrived for her first meeting with the teacher. Her three-year-old son Aaron would be starting school the following week. The teacher outlined the first week's schedule, explaining that he welcomed and expected Mrs. K. to stay in the classroom with Aaron. He invited Mrs. K. to the first parents' meeting, which was being held that evening. (Mrs. K. had already received an invitation in the mail.)

"How are you feeling about Aaron's beginning school?" the teacher asked.

"Well, to tell you the truth," Mrs. K. answered, "I'm excited. It's wonderful to see him becoming so independent and so grown up. But I'm a little nervous, too. You know it's a new phase in our lives. I'm so used to leaving him at home with the babysitter when I'm at work. And I don't think my boss will let me take the day off to stay in the classroom."

"Other mothers have told me the same thing. So you can see that you're not alone in your feelings. Do you think your babysitter, or someone who knows your son well, could stay with him for a time in the beginning?"

"Well, I'm sure he'll be fine without me, but I suppose that the sitter, or my mother, could spend some time with him to help him get used to it here."

The teacher and Mrs. K. have just started to build their relationship. The teacher raised the issue of separation so that Mrs. K. would have the opportunity to prepare herself and her son. He tried to make Mrs. K. feel that her slight nervousness and her inability to stay were not unusual. Mrs. K. was trying to make the teacher feel that her son would be a "good boy." The groundwork had been set for the teacher and parent to begin to work together.

Had it been possible for this parent to stay with the child, if she worked evenings or part time, or was a full-time homemaker, the teacher would have worked out a transition to the classroom that would fit the schedule of the parent. The important aspect of these arrangements for beginnings is flexibility. A rigid method tends to create conflicts and misunderstanding.

CHILDREN ARE STRANGERS

When children come to school for the first time, they are strangers. You know very little about them. They know very little about you. You have not had time yet to become sensitive to their cues. You have not become alert yet to that "look in Tina's eyes" telling you that a storm may break.

During these beginning days you may have very little information to guide you, for children have many different ways of telling you how they feel. Each one has his or her own behavior vocabulary. For example, two children may feel angry. One child may scream in rage; another may withdraw into a quiet, sullen shell. As you come to know the children by means of your observations and your contact throughout the year, you begin to know which behavior, for which child, means what most of the time.

Perhaps you depend on your intuitions and on your former experiences to cope with the range of feelings that you see a child express. Sometimes you will probably be right in what you surmise and what you decide to do. Sometimes you will probably be wrong. Much of what you do in the beginning will be guesswork. For that reason, it is crucial at a child's entry to enlist support of the parents, who truly know the child best.

PARENTS AS A SOURCE OF INFORMATION

The first meeting with parents, held before or as children begin in your program, is vital for learning about the children. It will establish the tone of your working relationship with the family and will influence the nature of your exchanges throughout the year. You and the parents will each begin to form an opinion of one another. It is up to you to set this tone by your friendliness, your openness, and your ability to listen and to withhold judgment.

In this first exchange, you will be able to learn about the parents' concerns and wishes for their children. The parents will be able to sense your interest in them as well as your interest in their sons and daughters.

Important information about children can be gleaned from this first meeting by posing thoughtful questions for parents such as

What made you seek day care (or nursery school) at this time?
What are your wishes and aspirations for Brian?
What would you like me to know about Sarah's development?
What can you tell me about Alex's pattern of eating and sleeping?
    About his usual routine at home?

How would you describe Maria's personality and disposition? What do you like most about her? Is there anything about her that you would like to change?

Your task in this first interview will be twofold: first, to learn what the parents think about their children by listening carefully to how they talk about them, and second, to help parents think about their decision to send their children to day care or nursery school. You can do this by describing your program and the nature of your school or center so that parents can decide whether or not they have made the right choice.

PROVIDING HELP FOR PARENTS AND CHILDREN WHEN SCHOOL BEGINS

You can reassure parents that you welcome them to stay with their children for the beginning day or days, or as long as they believe it necessary. While some parents may worry that they will not be allowed to stay at all, others may worry that they will be required to stay too long or that their children will never stay unless they leave the school immediately.

Here are some ways in which you can help parents strike a balance—neither too short nor too long a stay.

Discuss the entry process and raise the issue of separation in your initial interview, either when the parent seeks information about the school or before school starts. If feasible, reinforce this with a phone call before the child arrives for the first day. Perhaps the parent has last-minute questions or concerns.

Be a good listener. What are parents really saying? Are they nervous about separation? Are they receptive to your ideas? Do they minimize the impact of separation? Are they reluctant to participate in a separation process because they must go to work or because they reject the concept itself? Do they need more information? Are they concerned that their children will never separate if they stay in the room? Do they suggest "slipping out" while the children are occupied? You must decide how you will handle these questions. Some of them are discussed later in the chapter.

Reassure parents that you will work as partners with them for the benefit of their children. You can let them know that you will take your cues from them since they know their children best. Some parents may need to hear that you will not require them to stay any longer than necessary, especially if a child has been in a program before—or if he or she is the second, third, or fourth child in the family.

Have a plan for the first week, or weeks, based on the age and needs of the children and the needs of the parents. The younger the children, the more time will probably be needed for them to feel safe. A plan that is worked out with the entire staff of the school or center offers consistency to parents. Chapter 6, on school policy, contains some guidelines for forming such plans.

Support parents when it is impossible for them to attend with their children and have a plan to communicate with them each day of the entry period. Sometimes an additional daily phone call or two from the parent at work to the child at the center helps bridge the gap.

When you provide supportive help to parents, in most cases they will respond with information about themselves and their children that will contribute to your effectiveness. You will learn from them through the support and help you give them.

PARENTS IN THE CLASSROOM

Further support for your efforts to learn about the children from their parents will come through the parents' presence in your classroom during the first days of the children's attendance. Parents have intimate information about their children, such as the following:

> He'll stay by my side for a while watching what the other children do, but then he'll make his way over to something that interests him.
>
> She's such a social butterfly! You'll see that in no time at all she'll be talking up a storm with another child.
>
> We're really going to have trouble with Randy. He never wants me to leave him. I don't know what I'm going to do.

Other parents may be more circumspect about what they say to you, in their efforts, perhaps, to gain your approval. The range of communicated information is wide in any given classroom.

PARENTS CONTRIBUTE TO CHILDREN'S SECURITY

Research has shown that children are more exploratory and more openly social in an unfamiliar environment if they are accompanied by a familiar adult, usually a parent (Arsenian, 1943; Cox & Campbell, 1968; Rheingold & Eckerman, 1971). However, these children behaved quite differently in the same strange environment when their parents were not there. Rather than investigating the objects in the environment and exploring the space, some children showed distress by crying, thumb sucking, or stamping their feet. Others spoke less, stopped playing, or moved about hesitantly. With the familiar adult present, the children played, spoke, and moved about comfortably. Apparently the adults' presence was a secure base from which the children could wander, explore, and return. These studies have been interpreted to mean that the adults' presence communicated a feeling of power to the children, while the adults' absence conveyed powerlessness.

You can probably translate these research findings into your own life. Have you ever had the feeling, when embarking alone on a new adventure, that you would rather have the company of a familiar person? Is it more comfortable for you to walk into a room full of strangers with another, known person than by yourself? Do you remember going to college and feeling that you would like to have one of your family members or a close friend with you, at least for a short time? Did you ever long for the comfort of your old home after you moved to a new location? These natural longings for familiarity in new and untried situations are a part of our human heritage.

Though young children feel safer with their parents near by, they also have a great push from within to steer their own ship. "You're not the boss of me!" the four-year-old cries out against adult authority. "I do it myself!" the two-year-old shouts at offers of help. These conflicting tides are unsettling to children as well as to adults. While one urge pulls the child toward adult protection, the other propels the child away into a sea of her own actions. Even we, as adults, may experience conflicting feelings—wanting and simultaneously not wanting to be separate, independent, and autonomous; wanting and at the same time not wanting to be connected to or merged with another person.

TEACHERS ALSO EXPERIENCE CONFLICT

Is it any surprise that when children enter our classrooms, torn between wanting to leave their parents and wanting to hold on to them, that teachers, too, get caught up in the age-old dilemma? "The maturing adult," Louise Kaplan (1978) writes in *Oneness and Separateness*, "is continually reliving and revising his memories of childhood, redefining his identity, reforging the shape of his selfhood, discovering new facets of his being" (p. 32). This conflict between wanting to be autonomous and wanting to be dependent exists to some degree in all adults. Surely you have felt that pull between the feeling that "I'd just like to go to bed, pull the covers over my head, and forget everything" and the feeling that "I can take care of it." These adult feelings have some similarity to the contrary pulls that children experience, especially when they enter school.

Recognition of this conflict is the important and necessary first step for teachers. Young children and parents need help resolving this conflict when children begin school. It is a heavy burden that falls on the teacher's shoulders.

While young children need their parents to help them make a comfortable transition from home to school, teachers often wish this were not so. "If only those parents would get out of the room, I could get on with my work with the children." How often we hear that said! Sometimes school rules serve this purpose.

> Children are to ride the bus on the first day. Seats are for children only.
> Parents bringing children on the first day may stay for the first half hour.

Such regulations send strong messages to parents that they are not wanted.

Yet parents have feelings about their children's first days at school or group care that need to be recognized and supported by teachers. Parents also need to have control over their children's lives and to have a say in how their children will make the transition to school. Rules that keep them out deny them this control, as do rules that dictate overly structured entry schedules. How to arrive at an entry procedure that meets the needs of each parent and child is a challenging problem. How you work with parents in the first days will contribute to a spirit of either cooperation or competition. If you are receptive to learning from parents in the beginning days, your relationships can develop productively. Parental information will provide the fine tuning you need as you turn your attention to learning from children.

USING A QUESTIONNAIRE

In addition to talking with parents you may wish to consider using a questionnaire. One advantage of a questionnaire is the time for reflection that it offers—both to the person answering it and to the person reading it. On the other hand, all the questions may not be suitable for all groups of parents. Furthermore, it may not be appropriate to ask some parents to fill it out, if they are non-English speaking, for example, or if they are inexperienced with questionnaires.

In cases where you choose not to ask the parents to fill it out, you might use the questionnaire as a guide for your conference, going over questions you feel are pertinent. You may find that some questions are inappropriate for parents of different cultures, and you may decide to omit those questions or substitute others.

If you do choose to have parents fill it out, it would be best for you to ask the parent directly to do so. If you make home visits, you might leave it with the parent at that time, describing generally the kinds of questions it contains. You might prefer to wait a few weeks, until you know the parent and child better, to ask that a questionnaire be answered.

Since people react differently to questionnaires, it is important to emphasize with parents that the answers they provide will help you know their children better and improve your work with them in school.

Here are some questions you might ask yourself as you evaluate the questionnaire for your use:

Will parents need help in understanding why I want to know some of these facts?

Would it be better to fill out this questionnaire together with the
parent? Would this provide a good basis for our conference?
Would it be better to do it with both parents rather than one?
How can I make good use of the answers? What do the answers
tell me about the child? About the parents?
What shall I do with information that indicates the parents have a
very different attitude from mine about child rearing?

You will find a sample questionnaire for parents at the end of this
chapter.

A PARENTS' MEETING BEFORE SCHOOL OPENS

A parents' meeting held before school begins can ease the initial
phase of school entry. This may be more difficult to accomplish in a
day care setting where children enter at varied times during the year.
It can be done, however, within three months of entry dates.

A meeting focusing on school beginning and the separation of parent and child validates for parents that this is an occasion meriting
attention. If held in the evening, such a meeting makes it possible
for working parents who hold daytime jobs outside the home to attend.
Providing refreshments and name tags helps to loosen the tensions
people feel when they participate in a group consisting mainly of
strangers. Though you, the teacher, may be familiar with many who
are attending, most of the parents probably will not know one another.
One of the positive aspects of a meeting for parents is their making
contact with other parents of young children. Thus the meeting provides both a social and an educational function.

> I liked having other parents who, as I gradually got to know them, I could
> learn from and talk with about the progress and process of being parents
> and raising children. (A parent's response to my questionnaire)

The meeting can have several different components. Inviting several "old" parents to speak about their experiences and feelings at the
beginning of the year sets a tone of sharing and comfort. Displaying
the work of children from past years—their paintings, drawings, clay
work, wood constructions—lends a flavor encouraging the parents'

positive anticipation. Quotes from children indicating how they managed the entry process would be reassuring for new parents. Photographs showing children entering school or a slide presentation would help to make the process concrete and tangible. Mentioning books to read to children about school and about separation might be a welcome aid for parents (see appendix A for a list of recommended texts). Some of the suggestions in chapter 4 can be shared with parents, especially the listed criteria for choosing good books. Preparing a booklist to hand out and making copies of some books available on display or for borrowing would be a cooperative and supportive action. It would be important to tell parents to read these stories as they would read any stories, in a context that is relaxed and enjoyable.

The tone of the meeting will take shape mainly from the sort of person you are. If you are by nature a relaxed, informal person, your meeting will take on those characteristics. If, on the other hand, you are more formal and more comfortable with set structure, your meeting will reflect these preferences. Your prior experience as a group leader will also dictate how your meeting goes. If this is your first meeting it will, without doubt, be less successful in your eyes than if this is your third or fifth or tenth meeting.

Perhaps the most important feature of the meeting will be the sharing parents do with one another. This meeting should not be a lecture. Meetings designed to encourage a maximum amount of group participation are considered one of the most effective techniques for adults (Berger, 1981). Such active group discussions provide the following benefits:

> They help those taking part to clarify their thinking, and to integrate their thoughts with those of others.
> Hearing the experiences of others gives parents some perspective on and help in solving many of their problems.
> Parents gain a better understanding of their children and themselves through the discussion of common problems.
> Through participation in group thinking, parents not only acquire knowledge but often come to feel differently about things.

Group discussions are facilitated by the physical arrangement of people in the room. If parents are seated in a circle, they are most likely to talk to one another as they exchange ideas. Conversely, if they are seated in rows, they are more likely to address their remarks to the teacher who is leading the group, because they do not make eye contact with other parents as easily. You will need to decide which arrangement furthers the goal you have in mind for your meeting.

Giving information about the beginning days may be an important aspect of this first meeting. Even though you may have mailed out written information about your entry procedure (see appendix B for a sample), you may want to discuss your policy with parents. This provides an opportunity for them to raise questions and concerns about your procedure. It also opens up the topic of separation and encourages parents to express their feelings about leaving their children.

In one such parents' meeting, a father asked, "How does it go for parents when you say good-bye at the center as opposed to saying good-bye at home?" He seemed worried that his daughter might have different feelings about being left at home and being left at the center.

The teacher in this case was very experienced with school beginnings and gave a long, explicit answer:

> Everyone has a different way of saying good-bye. You and I can talk about how you say good-bye at your house, and I can learn from you. There's no set answer about how we say good-bye here, but we do ask you to say good-bye. What we want is to make links with home before you say good-bye here. You'll provide pictures of yourselves to hang on our wall. I will send a letter to the children telling them that I am waiting to see them. You'll be talking with the children at home about the center. You'll be teaching us about your children. We have already learned that Katherine is called Katie; that George carries the corner of an old blanket to every new place. We also make home visits. We get to know that your cat is black, where the kitchen is, what's in your child's room.
>
> We'll ask you to stay close to the building when you first say good-bye, and we'll ask you to come back soon. Everyone will be on an individual schedule. It's not step by step. It's a process; it goes on all year. There will be give and take between the teachers and the parents.

The teacher's answer seemed reassuring to many of the parents, and they felt free to begin asking questions. Since this was an all-day program, people asked questions about naps, about the various activities in which the children would be involved, about schedules for eating, for playing, for going outdoors, for sleeping. There was concern for going home time: "Do all the children think it's time to go when the first child is picked up?"

The teacher did not immediately answer all questions directly. Often she encouraged other parents to give an opinion if it seemed appropriate, or she asked parents to raise other, related questions, and then she answered them together. In that way parents began to share their concerns with one another. They found out that they were not alone in their worries.

Here are some of the questions parents wanted to discuss:

How long will it take before my son can stay without me?

What do you do if a child cries a lot?

My daughter is used to my leaving for work. Can my sitter bring her to school?

My boy has never been left with anyone outside the family. How long will it take for him to get used to the center?

Will there be an opportunity for me to tell you some things about her eating preferences and habits?

The answers you provide for parents will depend on the design for beginnings that you have evolved. If you have constructed a plan that includes a home visit, a gradual and staggered entry, a slow-paced phasing-in period, an individual approach to each parent-child style of separating, a place for parent conferences or mini-conferences, and a general belief in the importance of this separation event, you will be able to reassure parents and support their efforts to encourage their children's positive growth and development. There is a good chance that both children and parents will emerge from this experience feeling that they have been cared for and nurtured at a time when they needed it most. It is easier for parents to cope with a difficult situation when they feel supported and encouraged.

FATHERS AND CHILDREN

Not all conferences and parental contact are with mothers. While the word "parent" is still largely equated with women in this society, it is a growing reality that many men are deeply involved in the day-to-day care of their children. There are those who share child care with women and those who have sole responsibility for the rearing of their children. Your own attitudes toward men as nurturers will partially develop from the amount of experience you have had with men as caretakers of young children.

During the past decade the role of the father has started to change profoundly. Many men are exploring new ways to express both their masculinity and nurturance, a combination that has not existed traditionally in this country. As one father wrote: "One of the most significant changes in fathering today is the recognition that fathers need not be bound by the traditional roles handed down by their fathers and grandfathers. . . . They want to balance and integrate the provider/protector role with the nurturer/caregiver role" (Franklin, 1983, p. 9).

This shift in role has produced conflict for many men, and they often experience ambivalence about the meaning of masculinity. At

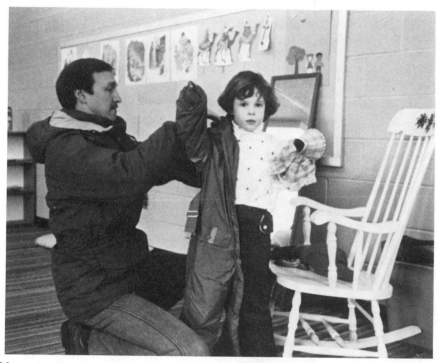

How do you react to men as caretakers of children?

the same time, both men and women have mixed feelings about men who are taking on a new role. Caretaking men are often regarded as less than masculine or their work is viewed as unimportant.

A significant aspect of the recent studies on fathers is that children are more attached to fathers than had previously been acknowledged. Fathers have been shown to find school separations stressful (Bloom-Feshbach, Bloom-Feshbach, & Gaughran, 1980; Hock, McKenry, Hock, Triolo, & Stewart, 1980). The implications for teachers are obvious. Fathers need as much empathy and attention during the separation process as do mothers and children, and fathers can be effective in helping children adjust to the new situation.

Marcus, aged four, stood outside the classroom door, refusing to come in, burying his face and body in his father's legs. The teacher encouraged them to enter, but short of dragging Marcus in, it was clearly impossible. The teacher left the door open and encouraged the father to stay there with Marcus, for the short first-day session. She repeatedly made contact with them, speaking encouraging words to the father in her attempt to help him find comfort in this uncomfortable situation.

The next day, the teacher and Marcus' father decided that he would carry Marcus into the room. Mr. C. sat in a chair with Marcus on his lap. Marcus hid his face on his father's shoulder and closed his eyes, refusing to look at the room or the teacher who tried to play a peek-a-boo game with him. The teacher shared Mr. C.'s discouragement but urged him to continue to come to the classroom the next day.

When Mr. C. arrived on day three, Marcus was willing to walk in with him and again sit on his lap. As long as Mr. C. kept his arms around Marcus, he was willing to sit up and look around. Although the teacher smiled and spoke to them both many times during the shortened morning session, Marcus remained stony-faced and still. The teacher reminded Mr. C. that progress had been made since the first morning and communicated her faith that eventually Marcus would let go of his father and come to school.

The next few days proved her right. Her continuing support of Mr. C. and her reaching out to Marcus allowed him gradually to slip from lap to floor, from standing next to his father to sitting at a table with a puzzle, to painting, to engagement with the teacher, and finally to interacting with other children.

Mr. C. and the teacher built a strong relationship in those first few days. While Mr. C. continued to be an important person to Marcus, the boy finally was able to transfer some of his trust from his father to the teacher.

Until recently men have been neglected in the child development literature (Lamb, 1981), and thus few books for teachers have included a point of view about fathers. With increasing numbers of men becoming involved in the daily care of their children, and with increasing numbers of men entering the early childhood profession, it is a matter of some urgency that teachers of young children think about the implications of this.

How comfortable are you in your dealings with fathers, both in staying with their children in your classroom and in holding conferences with them?

Give some thought to your own rearing. How did you, as a child, regard the role of men in bringing up children? Can you identify any remains of those old feelings that shape your present attitudes?

When a father, rather than a mother, picks up his son or daughter at the end of a session, is your behavior the same or different? If different, do you know in what way it is different? And why?

What have been some of your successful communications with fathers? You may wish to make a list to share with your co-workers.

The absorption of fathers and men in the lives of young children is a trend gaining much momentum and is adding richness to the lives of all.

VARIED APPROACHES TO HELPING PARENTS

Sometimes the entry and separation procedure do not go smoothly. Some children and parents have a difficult time. These difficulties take many different forms, and while there may be elements of similarity from one relationship to the next, no two parent-child pairs are exactly alike in the way they cope. Because of this, there are various ways to help parents through this time—different things to say, different approaches to take.

Parents look to the teacher to help them know what to do. You may need to make decisions with several parent-child pairs and each may be unique.

Ms. G. was clearly shocked and angry when her child screamed and cried as she attempted to leave her in the center. "I think she's pulling an act," Ms. G. told the teacher.

"Why do you suspect that?" the teacher asked.

"Well, she's never done anything like this before. She never cries or anything when I go to work and leave her at her grandmother's."

As the teacher and mother discussed Maria's behavior, the mother revealed that she had never left three-year-old Maria in any strange place before. Ms. G., however, thought it was an "act" and that Maria should straighten out and stay in school without such a big fuss. Besides, Ms. G. had to go to work and couldn't be spending long hours at the center.

The teacher, recognizing Ms. G.'s need to leave for work, supported her leaving, and reassured her that she would take good care of Maria.

"Children frequently cry and cling to their mothers when they are left in a new place. They're frightened and worried about themselves. We understand that in this center and we'll do everything we can to help Maria feel safe. We'll hold her and play with her. Why don't you call us when you have a break at work and we'll tell you what's going on here. You can talk to Maria, too. She might cry when she hears your voice, so prepare yourself. What it means is that she loves you and misses you. But the phone call is important for her. It's a way of telling her that you're still o.k. and that you love her and you will be back."

Perhaps Maria's mother pretended that she did not expect Maria to behave that way because she was afraid that the teacher would not accept Maria into her center. On the other hand, perhaps she was genuinely surprised. Whatever the case, Ms. G. needed the teacher's help just as much as Maria did. Telling Ms. G. to phone when she got to work was a way of informing her that the teacher is on her side and that the teacher knows how worried she feels, even if she never said so.

Sometimes parents are angry at the teacher for suggesting that they stay with their child. They take it as an insult. This makes some teachers very defensive. Teachers sometimes feel that they are trying to make life "nice" for the child and the parents are giving them a hard time.

What should you do? It seldom helps to get into a verbal battle with a parent at that point, especially when the child so clearly needs the parent to be there. This may occur despite the fact that the parent has received all the information about school entry that other parents have. It is important for you to be firm without being angry.

I can see that you're uncomfortable here with Nikki and that you'd prefer
to leave. I can understand your feeling of wanting to go when she clings
that way. But it's so common for children to act that way at this age—we
pretty much expect it here at school. She truly seems to need you and
isn't ready yet to accept me. Do you have any suggestions for how I might
get to know Nikki—things that she particularly likes to do and could do
with me so that she'll come to trust me and feel safe here?

The teacher has tried to enlist Nikki's mother in the solution of
this problem and help her become responsible for the comfort of her
own child. The teacher has set a tone of cooperation as well as empow-
erment for the parent.

If the parent insists on leaving, the teacher might also ask, "Who
else takes care of her? Might that person be able to spend some time
with her in school?"

You may notice a child who has some worries about staying in
school and want to share that information with his or her parent.
Often mini-conferences, especially at pick-up time, seem to take place
in a natural way. Here is how one teacher used those informal times
in a positive way:

I have had many mini-conferences with Angela's mother in which we both
shared our concern about Angela's reticence. Ms. R. really tuned in during
these conferences, and we did some good teamwork. For several weeks,
Ms. R. took Angela out of school at noon so that they could have lunch
together and she could give Angela more focused, intimate talking time.
In the classroom, I tried to give Angela the support and encouragement
she needed, and she seems finally to be coming into her own. She seems
to be feeling stronger about being Angela, and I think she is ready to use
language more abundantly.

Some parents need help in leaving a child in a way that is helpful
to the child, such as the mother who holds her child on her lap for
long periods of time, or the father who leaves, then returns in a few
minutes, leaves again but peers through the classroom window for a
long time. It often relieves parents who seem so ambivalent if you
are honest with them:

You seem to be having trouble making up your mind about whether Katie
should be here or not. A lot of parents feel that way—they want their
children to have a good time in school, but at the same time they feel

unhappy about the fact that the children are growing up or spending time away from them. Would it help if you went out for half an hour or an hour and then came back? We could increase the time out of the room each day until you both feel comfortable. Why don't you tell me when you're ready to do that?

Some teachers provide a coffee pot in the hall or in another room for parents during these beginning days to help them when they begin to take short leaves from the room.

Sometimes parents are concerned about leaving their children but do not share those feelings with the teacher. This might be because they, themselves, are shy or because they believe that the teacher may see them as interfering in the classroom life. If you sense that a parent may need support, you may find that discussing it helps to clear the air.

Mr. L. was often directive toward Marc and toward the teachers as well. The teacher felt that perhaps Mr. L. needed reassurance that Marc was being looked after in school. When she asked him how he felt about leaving Marc with her, he told her that he felt a little apprehensive because Marc is so quiet and undemanding that sometimes he could be overlooked. The teacher assured Mr. L. that she would take good care of Marc and that she was very fond of the boy. The teacher recognized that quiet children can, indeed, be overlooked.

Once in a while you may find that after a suitable period of time a child is ready to move out on his own but the parent is not. It may be hard for the parent to say that final good-bye and leave the room. This frequently annoys teachers. Some empathy might provide a key:

It seems to be hard for you to say good-bye to Elysa. I wonder if we can make a plan that will make it more comfortable for you.

Sometimes a little humor is needed to lighten the mood:

It looks like we've gotten Elysa settled, and now it looks as if we've got to help you settle, too! How can we go about it?

Teachers help young children and their parents to separate comfortably by communicating a sense of understanding and belief in their own ability to support the separation process. Parents' worries

(*Continued on page* 92)

Elaine Wickens

Nils is uncomfortable knowing that his mother is about to leave. He frets when the teacher tries to comfort him.

He returns to his mother for comfort from his distress,

Elaine Wickens

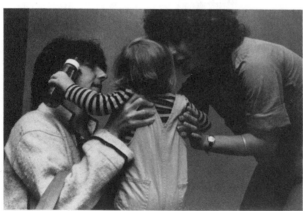

Elaine Wickens

but she needs to leave. She gives him to the teacher who receives him affectionately and with understanding.

His mother is gone.

"It's sad when a mom has to leave her little boy," the teacher says consolingly.

Gently she helps him into water play at the sink, reassuring him with her words and her presence.

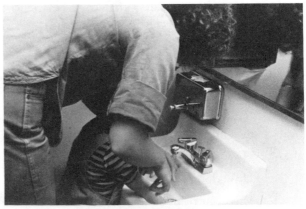

are lessened when they sense that teachers have faith that they will be able to care for the child competently and the parent is able to see that demonstrated daily. It is trying for parents to leave a sobbing child with the teacher, even though it may be the second or even the third month of school. The teacher who recognizes that the separation process takes time and effort can share that with the parent through actions that may be more powerful than words.

There is no way to foresee all the possible reactions to separation that the parents and children may experience and to give suggestions for them all. Basically what happens between you and the parents of the children in your room will depend on you—how you view parents, and how you regard separation. You are the person who sets the tone in any interaction with parents.

QUESTIONNAIRE FOR PARENTS: FOCUSING ON SEPARATION

This questionnaire has been designed to help you know more about the children who will be entering your classroom for the first time. It may alert you to possible reactions a child may have when leaving the parent becomes a reality. It is also designed to alert the parent to the possibility that his or her child may need attention and care when going through this particular event. It is not a scientifically perfected instrument, nor is it meant to be. Rather, it is a guide to help you and the parents focus upon some aspect of the child's experiences and personality that may relate to the entry and separation process. Its purpose is to sensitize you and the parents to the meaning of children's behaviors at this time.

It is based, in part, on the "Parental Anxiety Rating Scale" reported in the work of Doris, McIntyre, Kelsey, & Lehman (1971).

1. How old was your child when you first left him/her with a sitter or someone other than you?

   How did s/he react at that time?

   How does s/he react now?

   Have there been any changes in the people who take care of him/her?

If yes, how does s/he react to those changes?

How do you feel when you leave him/her with another person for care?

2. Does your child have a favorite blanket or toy to which s/he is attached?

   Under what circumstances does s/he use it?

3. How does your child react to people s/he does not know, either in or outside your home?

4. Has your child ever been left accidently for a brief time, such as in the supermarket?

   If yes, how did s/he react?

5. How does your child behave when s/he is asked to mix with a new group, such as at a birthday party?

6. Has your child ever stayed overnight at the home of a friend or relative?

   If yes, describe his/her reactions to the experience.

7. Have either or both parents been away overnight or for a period of time?

   If yes, how old was the child at the time?

   How did s/he react to this separation?

   Who cared for him/her at that time?

8. Has your child ever been hospitalized?

   If yes, at what age?

   For what reason?

   For what length of time?

   Were parents allowed to stay with the child?

   Describe the circumstances, including his/her reactions to this hospitalization.

   How did s/he behave when s/he came home?

9. Was either parent ever hospitalized?

   For what length of time?

   What was the child told?

   Was s/he permitted to visit?

   What were his/her reactions?

10. Has there been a death of anyone close to your family, or of a pet?

    If yes, what was the child's relationship to that person?

    What was s/he told?

    What were his/her reactions to the death?

11. If you and your spouse have been separated or divorced, what is the living arrangement for your child?

    What has been his/her reaction to this situation?

    In what way do you think it will affect his/her entry into school and his/her separation from you?

12. Have you moved during the child's lifetime?

    If yes, how many times?

    How old was s/he?

    How did s/he react to the move?

13. What does your child do when s/he is angry?

    Afraid?

    Sad?

    Happy?

14. What makes your child fearful?

15. How does your child recover from emotional stress?

16. How do you think your child will react to beginning school?

    How do you think s/he will react when you leave him/her in school without you?

17. What does your child like to do that may help us plan activities for him/her?

18. What are your child's favorite games? Storybooks? Toys?

19. What else would you like us to know about your child that would help us in planning for his/her most comfortable entry into school and the most comfortable separation for both of you?

6

Making School Policy

For the adequacy to be felt, separation must be implemented, must be successful. Thus separation... was no longer considered a problem; a special case. Separation became a part of the very reason and service of nursery school, what nursery school does. (Weber, 1959, p. 45)

All schools and centers have a point of view about school entry and separation, whether they ignore them or make plans for them. If they ignore them, then most likely their point of view is based on the traditional stance that separation is not an event of special importance and that to drop a child and run is best for everyone concerned. If schools plan for separation, they are acknowledging the significance of the attachment between parents and children. There are many degrees of this acknowledgment. They range from prescribing that parents stay only the first day to planning individually to meet the differing needs of each parent-child pair.

This text reflects the position that parent-child attachment is a basic necessity for healthy human development. Without the security of this attachment, children are limited in their capacity to become related human beings, capable of conceptual and creative activity. Helping children achieve a successful separation and adjustment to preschool settings is an incomparable opportunity for teachers. When children are able to master their separation feelings at school entry, they have achieved a giant step in their growth. This separation becomes "a healthy prototype for all the separations that will follow" (Furman, 1972, p. 234).

When a school regards entry and separation as an opportunity for growth, rather than as a problem, its policies will support this idea.

Teachers who believe in the effectiveness of their work concerning separation will be more supported and encouraged in schools or centers whose policies are consonant with their ideas. If your school's policies are not consistent with your developmental point of view, can you become an agent for change? What are some policies that identify school entry and the separation process as opportunities for children's growth?

A BROCHURE FOR PARENTS
AND A WELCOMING LETTER FOR CHILDREN

Many schools send to the parents a short description of what school-opening activities are and the reason why they are held. Look in appendix B for a sample of the brochure one school sends to all its parents. This brochure describes the school's philosophy about separation, attachment, and beginning days. It tells parents what to expect in the classroom during the early weeks of school.

With the brochure each classroom teacher might enclose a note, such as the following, addressed specifically to the girl or boy.

Dear Wayne:
    Soon your mom [dad, grandma, etc.] will be bringing you to our center [school]. We have so many things for you to play with here. When I see you, I will say, "Hello! I'm glad to see you here. I've been waiting for you."
                                                                    Your teacher,

PREOPENING "SPRUCE-UP" TIME

School policy might request a special "room spruce-up" in which new children and their parents can participate. While such an event is well suited to parent co-op schools, it can be adapted to other preschool programs. It would probably not be suitable for ongoing day care settings. A school might set aside one morning and/or one evening for such activities to accommodate working and nonworking parents who wish to attend. Teachers, parents, and children can work together setting playthings on shelves, washing or painting (using washable paint) pieces of equipment, readying tables and chairs, or performing other maintenance tasks. This would provide an opportunity for both children and parents to become familiar with the classroom, feel a sense of belonging, and also begin to know each other.

VISITS BEFORE SCHOOL OPENS

Schools may close for a day in the spring to allow children who will be attending the following fall to visit with their parents. This gives children a taste of the fun that is to come and provides a familiar reference point when they arrive for the first day in the fall. It enables parents to talk about the school with their children as they anticipate the first day. Parents, too, enjoy feeling familiar with a situation they are about to enter. A third advantage of this plan is that it is less disturbing to the ongoing class than a continual stream of visiting parents and children.

Preopening day visits can also be made in the fall before school officially starts. One school makes an appointment with each child and parent before opening day. They become acquainted with the room and the teacher. Children choose cubbies for clothing and belongings, and the teacher puts their names on them.

Here is the way a public school helps kindergarteners toward a smooth entry. The school administrative district in one town sent the following notice to parents in August concerning the bus schedule for the coming year:

Kindergarten: On Tuesday, September 1, each kindergarten teacher will be in the classroom from 1:00 to 3:00 P.M. Parents are invited to bring any children to meet his/her teacher. There will also be a school bus and driver at the school during the same hours for your child's familiarization.

Some of these suggestions are not suitable for day care centers. However, children can be brought for a short stay on the first day either by a parent or the person who has been caring for them. Many centers find that a slow start and the gradual addition of time over a period of a few days make a big difference in the comfort of children and the security of their parents.

A preopening visit does not replace the visits that parents need to make on their own when they search for an appropriate school or center.

PARENTS' MEETING BEFORE SCHOOL OPENS

When school policy includes such a meeting, as described in chapter 5, parents know that they have been seriously included in the plans for the opening of school.

HOME VISITS

Home visits can be part of a school policy, provided parents understand that they have the option to say no. Some parents do not feel comfortable about a teacher's visit and worry that the teacher may reject a child if he or she does not behave properly. Others welcome the visit as an opportunity to share a child's home life with a teacher. Likewise, some teachers may feel uncomfortable about such visits and need to be able to say no. Sometimes home visits are best arranged after school has been in session for a while and teacher and parents know each other a little better. One teacher took small groups of children, throughout the school year, to each of the children's home for juice and a snack by prearrangement with parents. All the children's homes were visited and working parents were able to plan in advance to be present.

Most children love to have their teachers visit and often talk about it even at the end of the school year.

STAGGERED ENTRY

Centers and schools frequently offer shortened hours, which are gradually lengthened during the first week or two of the program, to aid in school entry and separation. In establishing a schedule for gradual entry, keep in mind that returning children may generally require less time to settle in than first-time children. Children under the age of three will probably require a more gradual entry, especially those around age two, than children of four and five. As you make entry plans, take into account a child's previous experience: Has he or she been in group care before? Was that separation successful? Has she been home with a substitute caretaker? Does he have limited experience in activities outside the home?

In a day care setting it is most likely that you will have a core of children who continue to be with you when the new child or children arrive. Often the "old" children offer help to newcomers, which is an aid to, rather than a substitute for, your help. New children will usually look to you for the major part of their security in the beginning, especially since their parents will be gone for long hours and may have limited time to spend at the center.

An advantage of the staggered entry in a school where all the children begin at the same time is that the room is less crowded and parents, children, and teachers have more intimate access to one another. Three possible staggered entry plans are suggested as follows:

PLAN I (for a half-day program)

WEEK 1   *Monday, Tuesday, and Wednesday*
           9:00 to 10:00—half the class
           10:30 to 11:30—other half of class

           Thursday and Friday
           9:00 to 11:00—whole class

WEEK 2   *Monday through Friday*
           9:00 to 11:45—whole class, full session

PLAN II (for a full-day program)

WEEK 1   *First day*
           Children attend in groups of six for one hour.
           Six children and parents meet from 9:00 to 10:00, six from 10:00
             to 11:00, and six from 11:00 to 12:00.

           Second day
           Children and parents come in two groups of nine each.
           First group meets from 9:00 to 10:30.
           Second group meets from 10:30 to 12:00.

           Third, fourth, and fifth day
           All children attend together from 9:00 to 12:00.
           Parents stay as needed.
           No lunch served.

WEEK 2   *First day*
           Children who can separate stay all day.
           Others leave after lunch with parents.

Beyond this each child's adjustment is handled according to individual needs.

Within the first three weeks of school, the teacher will arrange a conference with each parent if possible.

PLAN III (for a full-day program)

WEEK 1   New and returning children and their parents come for one and a half hours for the first day. The rest of the week is devoted to individual schedules. Those who are able to separate stay until lunch, while others leave earlier.

WEEK 2   Individual plans are made, and children gradually stay for longer periods of time. Parents are encouraged to leave for varying amounts of time, according to the children's needs. Parents are asked to stay in the building until they and the teacher believe it is appropriate to go out. Returning children stay for lunch and nap as they work toward the full day. New children may require more time.

Home visits are made and conferences are held during the first two months.

ADJUSTMENT TO EATING AND SLEEPING

If the program includes lunch and a nap for very young children, these activities are often best added one at a time. Because sleeping and eating are potent reminders of home to young children, their feelings are often strongly aroused at those times. If parents accompany children when they eat in school for the first few times and as they nap in school in the beginning, it will ease the children's anxiety. Often children are afraid to sleep in an unfamiliar setting. Perhaps they are reluctant to relinquish the control they have while they are awake. Many children need to feel very safe before they give up that control and fall asleep.

A school policy that acknowledges the special nature of food and sleep in the life of young children will do much toward facilitating their growth toward independent functioning.

PARENTS IN THE CLASSROOM

When school policy requires that parents stay with their children during the first days of school, parents, children, and teachers can jointly attend to the work of separating. Such a policy attaches dignity and importance to starting school and resolves for parents any ambivalence they might have about whether or not they should stay. When there is no choice, parental anxiety is often greatly reduced. Such a policy might require other actions on the part of the school, such as providing adult-sized chairs in the classroom and a pot of coffee in the hall or in a separate room where parents might go when they begin to leave the classroom for short intervals.

Other policy issues will arise. Will you want parents to sit with their children in the activity areas or around the periphery of the room? What will you and a parent say to a child when the parent is about to leave the room?

It is important to tell a child, "Your mom has to leave now. She will be back right after we finish reading a story," or "Your dad is going now. When you wake up from your nap he will come back to take you home." Suppose a child wants to go with the parent? If this is a part-time program and the mother or father is going to another room for coffee, it might be reassuring for the child to see where that room is and to know that she can go there when she feels the need. On the other hand, if the mother is going to work and it is not possible for the child to go too, then honesty is crucial. "I know you'd like to leave with your mom, but she's going to work now and I will take good care of you while she's gone. She'll be back after our afternoon snack, you can depend on that."

How will you arrange your time so that you can observe parent-child interactions and also be supportive to parents when they are in need? This is never easy to accomplish—it is a little like juggling. Nevertheless, it is worth trying to figure out a plan for yourself so that you might be able to perform both functions.

"SNEAKING OUT"

What about the parent who "sneaks out," or wishes to, when his or her child is engaged in some activity? Often teachers comply with this request. Why? I suspect that it relieves both parent and teacher of the responsibility for saying good-bye. Often it is easier to avoid a problem than to face it. All of us, at times, harbor a bit of the "coward" within us. Yet in most cases when a parent disappears without telling a child, she usually senses the parent's absence quickly. How do children feel when they believe that a protecting parent is nearby, only to discover that he or she is missing? Abandoned? Fearful? Untrusting? These feelings are hardly a firm foundation on which to begin a new experience. Consider the impact of this situation on a child's perception of a parent and on the child's perception of you, the teacher, who has allowed this to happen. It must appear to children as deception rather than as trust. It is important to bring a parent back into the room should this happen without your knowledge and to explain, outside of the child's presence, why you oppose this practice.

As an adult you can probably understand children's feelings. For example, if a dentist told you he would be pulling a tooth, you would probably prepare yourself. If he started to pull it without telling you, you might be even more fearful. In addition, you might feel deceived. When you are told the truth, you are able to mobilize yourself to deal with the situation, no matter how difficult. In the coping you gain self-esteem.

It is similar for children. Having to deal with a painful event, and conquering it, brings gratification. When a child and parent say good-bye, the child and perhaps the parent may suffer some pain. The child who then struggles to overcome the pain, who finally, with the teacher's support, adjusts to school, takes a giant step toward self-confidence, self-reliance, and trust, and gains a large measure of self-control. When a parent sneaks out, however, his or her child is denied the opportunity to achieve such control.

SECURITY OBJECTS

Blankets, teddy bears, worn scraps of diapers, parent's handkerchiefs, nursing bottles, and such treasures are standard fare to which preschool children cling. A policy that smiles on these transitional objects says, in effect, "We know how it is when you're two, three, four, or five." It surely must feel comforting to young children when a teacher welcomes the stuffed animals and the blankets, allows children access to them at any time, and does not insist that they be shared.

A FINAL PARENT-SCHOOL GET TOGETHER

Just as school policy acknowledges the importance of separation at entry, it can, at the close of school, also acknowledge the importance of separation from the school, the teachers, and the other children. Partings are regarded as significant events in the lives of all who have been intimately connected to one another during the year. If your center is one that operates year round and there is no formal ending day, a school policy can be evolved that requires some form of recognition of a child's last day. Perhaps this could be a classroom party or a special lunch in which parents are invited to participate. Perhaps a picnic supper or a Saturday party could be arranged to mark the occasion. Giving departing children a booklet about their days in your program, perhaps including photos of each child engaged in a favorite activity or drawings by friends, often helps bring an ending to the present experience.

Ceremonies help people feel that closure has been made before they go on to something new.

WHAT ABOUT POLICY FOR CHILDREN
WHO ARE NOT READY?

A final consideration is children who demonstrate that they are not ready to leave home and not ready to enter into group life with other children. These children may be unable to engage themselves with materials or enter into activities; they may be unable to respond to comfort offered by teachers; they may be unable to respond joyfully to the events and people in the program. What policy will you set for such situations?

A policy that is flexible will serve parents and children best. You will need to consider the needs and feelings of the parent and child in question versus the needs of the group and your own capabilities. You will have to assess the child's potential for growth. Since there is no sure scientific measure available, you will need to make the most professional judgment possible. Perhaps the most valuable contribution you can make to the family in question will be that they not feel defeated or rejected. They need to feel supported and encouraged to believe that development in children takes time and that some

With our help children can evolve as confident, competent, and self-assured.

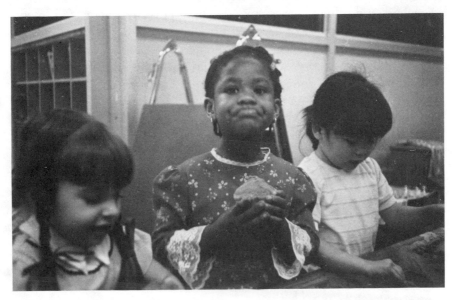

children take longer than others. If the situation is extreme, referral to psychological counseling may be indicated.

THE VALUE OF A SCHOOL POLICY
THAT SUPPORTS SEPARATION

It would be wonderful if all separations could be like this:

Kim's mom says good-bye at the door. Kim is standing with her back to her mother and the door, staring off into space. Hearing her mom's good-bye, she quickly turns and hugs her leg. Kim's mom stoops down, and Kim climbs into her lap. "I don't want you to go," Kim says in a quiet voice, peering intently into her mother's face. Her mom whispers in her ear, and Kim cheerily replies, "O.K. Have a good day." The mom stands up and Kim slides quickly behind her back doing a peek-a-boo movement as she breaks into a giggle. Her mom tells her she has to go. Kim asks earnestly, "What time are you coming?" Her mom reassuringly answers, "Three o'clock on the dot—after your afternoon snack." Her mom leaves, and Kim skips over to the easel.

However, since we know that there are many variations on this theme, we cannot expect that it will be like this for all children. Teachers and schools have a wonderful opportunity every fall to contribute to the growth of all children who enter their classrooms and to help them become truly self-reliant. Self-reliance in the fullest sense is based on the knowledge that they are not alone but that "standing behind them, there are one or more trusted persons who will come to their aid should difficulties arise" (Bowlby, 1973, p. 359). The mark of the truly self-reliant person is "a capacity to rely trustingly on others when occasion demands and to know on whom it is appropriate to rely" (p. 359).

In schools where policy and practice teach separation, more children will evolve as Kim did—confident, competent, and self-assured.

APPENDICES
REFERENCES
INDEX

APPENDIX A

Annotated Bibliography

FOR TEACHERS

Guides

Bernstein, J. *Helping children cope with death and separation: Resources for teachers* (Catalog 146). Urbana, Ill.: College of Education, University of Illinois, 1976.
> Contains an annotated bibliography that includes a selected list of books, films, filmstrips, and cassettes that treat death and separation.

Bernstein, J. *Books to help children cope with separation and loss.* New York: R. R. Bowker, 1977.
> In addition to a discussion of children's feelings about many kinds of separation and loss, this book gives guidelines for using books to help children cope. It also includes an extensive annotated bibliography of books for children through adolescence, plus a list of readings for adults.

Beyer, E. *Teaching young children.* Pegasus, N.Y.: Western Publishing Company, 1968.
> Supplies a sensitive section on teachers handling children's feelings concerning adjustment.

Curry, N. E., & Tittnich, E. M. Ready or not here we come: The dilemma of school readiness. Rev. ed. Paper presented at Arsenal Family and Children's Center Symposium celebrating National Week of the Young Child, Pittsburgh, Pa., May 18, 1972. (ERIC Document no. ED 168 729)
> Provides guidelines for assessing the school readiness of three- to six-year-old children. Discusses coping styles of children and the role of teachers and parents in the separation process.

Fassler, J. Children's literature and early childhood separation experiences. *Young Children*, 1974, 29, 311–23.
> Contains a list of books written specifically for the initial adjustment to school and the separation from parents. Those books fall into two categories: (a) reassuring stories to help contradict fears of abandonment, and (b) separation-type stories that might relate well to early school experiences. The article also includes books not related to school activities that deal with the issue of separation from parents that would be useful in school settings.

109

Discusses those books that are not helpful and mentions themes that have not received sufficient treatment in the juvenile literature, such as those emphasizing the ongoing relationship of a child and teacher.

Fassler, J. *Helping children cope: Mastering stress through books and stories*. New York: Free Press, 1978.

Describes and lists books that deal with a variety of separation experiences such as going to school, being left with babysitters, and going to sleep. The stories are those that help children gain a greater degree of mastery. Also discusses books that are not helpful.

Murphy, L. B., & Leeper, E.M. Preparing for change (no. 3). In L. B. Murphy & E. M. Leeper, *Caring for children series* (OED 75–1028). Washington, D.C.: U.S. Department of Health, Education, and Welfare, 1970.

Gives practical advice about helping children feel comfortable and safe during the beginning days of school. Also deals with the special problems of Monday mornings and returning to the center after an absence. Contains a section addressed to "When teacher is absent" and the situation of a new teacher taking over in the middle of the year.

Pacific Oaks College (Producer). *Mondays and Fridays*. Pasadena, Calif., 1975.

This filmstrip reveals the depth of children's feelings about separation and their fear of abandonment. Gives specific suggestions for easing the entry into day care. Audio cassette is in English on one side and Spanish on the other. Photographs show ethnically varied children, teachers, and parents.

Pitcher, E. G., & Ames, L. B. *The guidance nursery school*. Rev. ed. New York: Harper & Row, 1975.

Defines the problem of separation in the context of how the child handles new experiences. Offers suggestions to teachers about mothers' presence in the room and gradual withdrawal.

Read, K. H., & Patterson, J. *The nursery school and kindergarten: Human relationships and learning*. 7th ed. New York: Holt, Rinehart, & Winston, 1980.

Contains a section on helping children adjust to new experiences that focuses mainly on separation and school entry. Stresses potential for strengthening child's self-confidence, which lies in well-accomplished adjustment to school. Describes teacher's role with parents and children and is sensitive to teacher's feelings.

Rudolph, M., & Cohen, D. H. *Kindergarten and early schooling*. 2nd ed. Englewood Cliffs, N.J.: Prentice-Hall, 1984.

Offers practical suggestions to teachers on handling the adjustment to kindergarten.

Stein, S. B. *A child goes to school: A story book for parents and children together*. New York: Doubleday, 1978.

Presents photographic stories of a boy and a girl who go to kindergarten. Each story treats some form of separation, such as going to school for the first time, the death of a classroom pet, the departure of the teacher to have a baby, and the arrival of a new teacher to take her place. Each story is accompanied by a sound explanation of the meaning of the events to the child. While it is written for parents, it is just as useful to teachers.

Warren, R. *Caring: Supporting children's growth*. Washington, D.C.: National Association for the Education of Young Children, 1977.
> Contains a section called "Separation: A Developmental Challenge" that is sensitive to the feelings of children and parents and stresses the concept of mastery over fear as a positive step in growing up.

Works of Research and Theory

Archer, L., & Hosley, E. Educational program. In R. A. Furman & A. Katan (Eds.), *The therapeutic nursery school*. New York: International Universities Press, 1969.
> A description of the educational program of the Hanna Perkins School in Cleveland in which teachers and therapists worked with children and parents. Includes an explanation of the separation process and the uses of verbalization.

Berger, A. S. Anxiety in young children. *Young Children*, 1971, 27, 5–11.
> Describes the principle source of anxiety in early childhood as the loss of or separation from parents. Discusses the ways children deal with their fears.

Bloom-Feshbach, S.; Bloom-Feshbach, J.; & Gaughran, J. The child's tie to both parents: Separation and nursery school adjustment. *American Journal of Orthopsychiatry*, 1980, 50, 505–21.
> Investigates the interactions between maternal and paternal child-rearing styles and the child's mode of expressing separation distress during adaptation to nursery school. They found that the father-child relationship and the nature of the parental relationship were associated with the quality of nursery school adjustment. Case studies are particularly lively.

Bowlby, J. *Attachment and loss* (Vol. 1: *Attachment*; Vol. 2: *Separation anxiety and anger*). New York: Basic Books, 1969, 1973.
> Extensive review of studies and writings on the nature of attachment and separation and an explanation of Bowlby's theories of the innate process of attachment.

Bowlby, J. Attachment and loss: Retrospect and prospect. In S. Chess & A. Thomas (Eds.), *Annual progress in child psychiatry and child development: 1983*. New York: Brunner/Mazel, 1984.
> An historical sketch and a clear explanation of Bowlby's theory of attachment and the meaning of separation anxiety. Describes how he formulated his ideas based on observation of children.

Fraiberg, S. Separation crisis in two blind children. In R. S. Eisler, A. Freud, M. Kris, & S. L. Lustman (Eds.), *The psychoanalytic study of the child*, Vol. 26. New York: Quadrangle Books, 1972.
> Describes the meaning of separation to young children who cannot see and who had no adaptive solutions except regression, as opposed to sighted children who can be "active in the face of danger."

Furman, E. Mothers have to be there to be left. In A. Solnit, R. Eissler, A. Freud, & P. Neubauer (Eds.), *The psychoanalytic study of the child*, Vol. 37. New Haven: Yale University Press, 1982.
> An explanation of the varieties of feelings engendered in mothers when young children and infants begin to take growing-up steps that inevitably lead them

away from mother. The impact of this maturation on the part of the child has implications for the mother-child relationship.

Furman, R. Experiences in nursery school consultations. *Young Children*, 1966, *22*, 84–105.

A psychoanalyst describes his observations of the separation experiences of a three-and-a-half-year-old boy entering nursery school and returning the following year. He comments on how a nursery school for which he was a consultant recognized and handled the situation, enabling the child to achieve mastery of the separation experience.

Gross, D. W. On separation and school entry. *Childhood Education*, 1970, *46*, 250–53.

Discusses the nature of the child's problem-solving attempts when faced with the need to find a solution to separation at school entry. Describes the significance of entrance to school as a step toward growing up.

Gross, D. Separation: Problem or process. *Parents Press*, October 1979, p. 3.

Presents an insightful statement about the process of separation and its implications for the growth of the child.

Hirsch, E. S. *Problems of early childhood*. New York: Garland Publishing Company, 1983.

Discusses the meaning of separation experiences to children based on the work of Mahler, Bowlby, Winnicott, and Speers, as an introduction to a bibliography of books and articles for both adults and children. The annotated list contains a selection on entering school and has material on many other kinds of separation, such as parting from beloved people, sleeping away from home, being lost, losing a pet, and going to camp.

Hock, E.; McKenry, P. C.; Hock, M. D.; Triolo, S.; & Stewart, L. Child's school entry: A stressful event in the lives of fathers. *Family Relations*, 1980, *29*, 467–72.

In this study, forty fathers, whose children were, on average, five-and-a-half years old, were found to experience concerns about school entry and sadness at the separation. Families felt that they were not there to protect their children. Entry to school was found to be "stress provoking" for both mother and father.

Janis, M. G. *A two-year-old goes to nursery school: A case study of separation reactions*. New York: National Association for the Education of Young Children, 1965.

A detailed investigation of a two-year-old child at home and at school during her first year at nursery school. Examines the child's efforts at coping with separation distress and her eventual ability to make school "a place of her own, fulfilling needs and offering satisfactions away from home" (p. 120).

Kaplan, L. J. *Oneness and separateness: From infant to individual*. New York: Simon & Schuster, 1978.

Describes and defines the infant's psychological journey from a state of unity with the mother to a state of being a separate and unique self. Provides the reader with an in-depth portrait of the developing young child.

Katan, A. Some thoughts about the role of verbalization in early childhood. In R. S. Eissler, A. Freud, H. Hartmann, & M. Kris (Eds.), *The psychoanalytic study of the child*, Vol. 16. New York: International Universities Press, 1961.

The author makes three major points: (a) verbalization of the outer world precedes verbalization of feelings, (b) verbalization leads to an increase of the controlling function of the ego over affects and drives, and (c) verbalization increases the possibility of distinguishing fantasy from reality. She explains how verbalization leads to an increase in the child's mastery of feelings.

Kessler, J. W.; Gridth, A.; & Smith, E. Separation reactions in young, mildly retarded children. *Children*, 1969, *16*, 2–7.

Attributes separation anxiety in retarded children to their impaired ability to deal symbolically with the concept of the absent mother and to their impaired cognitive functioning. When the children were helped to separate by identifying themselves, their mothers, and their teachers as distinct individuals, they were able to separate and also to function more successfully.

Murphy, L. B. *The widening world of childhood: Paths toward mastery.* New York: Basic Books, 1962.

Describes the various coping styles of children when confronted with new and strange situations. Gives a detailed account of one child starting school and how he was helped by the efforts of his mother and teacher.

Provence, S.; Naylor, A.; & Patterson, J. *The challenge of daycare.* New Haven: Yale University Press, 1977.

A chapter on separation offers a developmental model for teachers. Describes what separation means to a child and to parents. Gives specific examples of how to alleviate distress and includes case histories.

Resch, R. C. On separating as a developmental phenomenon: A natural study. *Psychoanalytic Contemporary Science*, 1977, *5*, 207–69.

This study, based on natural observations of infants three months to three years old, shows how the capacity to separate from the mother and to develop modes of coping evolves from the small, daily life separations in familiar settings with familiar people. The study was done in an infant day care center in an urban community.

Robertson, J., & Robertson, J. Young children in brief separation: A fresh look. In R. S. Eisler, A. Freud, M. Kris, & S. L. Lustman (Eds.), *The psychoanalytic study of the child*, Vol. 26. New York: Quadrangle Books, 1972.

Acting as foster parents to four young children, one at a time, the authors compared the reaction to separation from their parents with that of a child left in a residential nursery. They found that the consistent care of one trusted person did not produce the protest, despair, and detachment described by Bowlby.

Rodrigues, D. T., & Hignett, W. F. Infant day care: How very young children adapt. *Children Today*, 1981, *10*(6), 10–12.

Report of a three-year study of ten children aged five to twenty-four months attending a day care center. Data showed that adaptation took place over time and that crying and protest occurred after the initial adaptation took place. They found that the most effective tool was helping both parents and caregivers understand the children's behavior and to know that the infant was reacting to internal stress and not to them. Specific suggestions are made for easing the child's transition from home to center.

Speers, R. W.; McFarland, M. B.; Arnaud, S.; & Curry, N. Recapitulation of separation-individuation processes when the normal three year old enters nursery school. In J. B. McDevitt & C. M. Settlage (Eds.), *Separation-individuation: Essays in honor of Margaret S. Mahler*. New York: International Universities Press, 1971.

> Describes the temporary regression in the behavior of normal children when they enter nursery school and the role of the mother in helping the child to adjust. Gives criteria to help mothers and teachers determine whether children are ready for school-linked separation.

Yarrow, L. J., & Pedersen, F. A. Attachment: Its origins and course. *Young Children*, 1972, 37, 302–12.

> Describes the nature of and the development of the attachment relationship between mother and child and sheds light on the understanding of the meaning of separation.

FOR PARENTS

Anderson, L. S. When a child begins school. *Children Today*, 1976, 5(4), 16–19.

> Gives helpful advice for parents of five- and six-year-olds by explaining both children's and parents' feelings. Lists some practical tips on how parents can help children and themselves when school begins.

Filstrup, J. M., with Gross, D. *Monday through Friday: Day care alternatives*. New York: Teachers College Press, 1982.

> The opening essay delves into the issue of separation, its psychology and its potential for growth. Through lively descriptions of actual situations, the other chapters illustrate a variety of child care arrangements.

Gotkin, J. Coping with separation anxiety: A new way to cut the apron strings. *Parents*, January 1977, pp. 35, 37, 60, 64.

> A parent writes about her experiences with her daughter when separation anxiety became a case of manipulation of the parents by the child.

Rogers, F. *When your child goes to school*. Pittsburgh: Family Communications, 1977.

> The author is Mr. Rogers of TV. The pamphlet is written for parents to share with children to ameliorate the discomfort of first days in school. The tone is reassuring and the suggestions are helpful, such as visiting the school beforehand.

Spock, B. When children are afraid to start school. *Redbook*, August 1975, pp. 22, 24, 27, 29.

> Advises parents on the meaning of children's fears at school entry and gives sound advice about ways to help ease the child's anxiety, such as previsits and getting young children used to strangers before they enter school. Addresses the topic of slipping out of the classroom unnoticed by the child.

Stein, S. B. *A child goes to school: A story book for parents and children together*. New York: Doubleday, 1978.

> Presents photographic stories of a boy and a girl who go to kindergarten. Each story treats some form of separation, such as going to school for the first time, the death of a classroom pet, the departure of the teacher to have a baby, and

the arrival of a new teacher to take her place. Each story is accompanied by a sound explanation of the meaning of the events to the child.

FOR CHILDREN

Adams, F. *Mushy eggs.* New York: G. P. Putnam's Sons, 1973.
When a beloved babysitter leaves two children for a job overseas, their sadness at her departure is touchingly expressed.

Amoss, B. *The very worst thing.* New York: Parents Magazine Press, 1972.
Depicts the feelings of a boy who enters school in midterm. At the end of the story he feels that the worst is over. For five- and six-year-olds.

Barkin, C., & James, E. *I'd rather stay home.* Milwaukee, Wisc.: Raintree Publishers, 1975.
A photographic story of a boy in a class of ethnically diverse children who overcomes his fear of starting school.

Binzen, B. *First day in school.* Garden City, N.Y.: Doubleday, 1972.
This photographic story shows a multicultural group of city children in their first day of kindergarten, feeling sad, frightened, and eventually happy and engaged in play.

Blue, R. *I am here: Yo esto aqui.* New York: Franklin Watts, 1971.
A young Puerto Rican girl must adjust to a new school, a new country, and a new language. She is helped by a warm assistant teacher who speaks Spanish.

Bram, E. *I don't want to go to school.* New York: Greenwillow Books, 1977.
Jennifer uses some stalling techniques because she is reluctant to go to kindergarten. Her patient and understanding mother helps her.

Brown, M. B. *Benjy's blanket.* New York: Franklin Watts, 1962.
Benjy grows from holding on to his baby blanket to his starting to forget it. He then resolves to give it to the new crying kitten next door.

Brown, M. W. *Goodnight, moon.* New York: Harper & Row, 1947.
A bunny ritually says goodnight to many objects in the bedroom, making the separation from the active daytime world into the dark, quiet sleeping world a comfortable transition. Bit by bit, the room gets darker as the bunny settles down to sleep.

Brown, M. W. *The runaway bunny.* New York: Harper & Row, 1972.
The familiar story of a little bunny who wants to run away. Fortunately, his mother won't let him. Written in a repeated pattern, this is a reassuring story of a mother's love and stability.

Burningham, J. *The blanket.* New York: Thomas Y. Crowell, 1975a.
For the very youngest children, this book shows the depth of the attachment to the security object, the upset at its possible loss, and the relief at its return.

Burningham, J. *The school.* New York: Thomas Y. Crowell, 1975b.
A little boy tells about the things he does in school. Could help start a discussion about beginning school. Simple text and drawings.

Carroll, R. *Where's the bunny?* New York: H. A. Walck, 1950.
A peek-a-boo story without words about a bunny who hides in funny places. The reader is the finder.

Chalmers, M. *Be good, Harry.* New York: Harper & Row, 1967.

A little cat reluctantly plays with a babysitter when his mother goes away. As she promised, his mother returns soon.

Cohen, M. *Will I have a friend?* New York: Collier, 1967.

A young child comes to preschool with his father and worries about finding a friend there. He does find one and his father says, "I thought you would."

Corey, D. *You go away.* Chicago: Albert Whitman, 1976.

The simple text says "You go away . . . and you come back" in a variety of separations involving children, men, and women of different ethnic groups. A mother hides behind a blanket and then reappears; two children lose sight of their mother in the supermarket; a little girl goes to kindergarten.

Eastman, P. *Are you my mother?* New York: Designer Books, Random House, 1960. (*Eres tu mi mama?* New York: Random House, 1967.)

A little bird falls from the nest and asks everyone, and everything, including a steam shovel, "Are you my mother?" In the end, the two are joyously reunited in a surprising way.

Harris, R. *Don't forget to come back.* New York: Alfred Knopf, 1978.

Annie tries everything to prevent her parents from leaving for the evening. Their calm assurance when the sitter arrives and their return prove her fear of abandonment groundless. A book to help spark a discussion of fears and feelings when being left.

Hill, E. *Where's Spot?* New York: G. P. Putnam's Sons, 1980.

A very simple text and large illustrations make this a good choice for very young children. It is a hide-and-seek book about a playful dog.

Hurd, E. G. *Come with me to nursery school.* New York: Coward, McCann, & Geoghegan, 1970.

Photographs in a multicultural nursery school setting show what children do there. This book can be used to prepare a child for school as well as to recount the joys of being there.

Kantrowitz, M. *Willy Bear.* New York: Parents Magazine Press, 1976.

A little boy prepares himself for his first day at school by pretending that it is Willy Bear who will be going. He conquers his fear and bravely bids good-bye to Willy.

Krauss, R. *The bundle book.* New York: Harper & Brothers, 1951.

An old favorite in which a little girl plays a game of peek-a-boo with her mother, told with a tone of affection and fun.

Lionni, L. *Little Blue and Little Yellow.* New York: McDowell, Obolensky, 1959.

This story is about two color daubs who are friends. They become green because they hug one another and then their parents don't recognize them. A happy reunion takes place when they return to their original blue and yellow colors.

Mannheim, G. *The two friends.* New York: Alfred Knopf, 1968.

A little girl feels shy, lonely, and fearful when she enters kindergarten. When she finds a friend she feels better. A photographic story about a black child and her supportive family.

Mayer, M. *Frog, where are you?* New York: Dial, 1969.

A story without words in which a boy and his dog awake one morning to find their pet frog gone. They search everywhere and finally find the frog.

Raskin, E. *Moose, Goose, and Little Nobody*. New York: Parents Magazine Press, 1974.
A small mouse cannot find his mother and is helped by Moose and Goose.

Rockwell, H. *My nursery school*. New York: Greenwillow, 1976.
How nursery school looks to the young child, told through a simple, well-illustrated book.

Simon, N. *I'm busy too*. Chicago: Albert Whitman & Company, 1980.
While their parents are busy working, three children are busy in school.

Soderstrom, M. *Maybe tomorrow I'll have a good time*. New York: Human Sciences Press, 1981.
Marsha Lou's first time in a day care center finds her bewildered and afraid. Her mother's return is reassuring. As she watches the other children she becomes more optimistic about the new opportunity before her.

Sonneborn, R. *Lollipop party*. New York: Viking, 1967.
The fearful feelings of a little boy who waits alone for his mother to come home are sensitively revealed.

Stecher, M. B., & Kandell, A. S. *Daddy and Ben together*. New York: Lothrop, Lee, & Shepard, 1981.
Daddy and Ben share a few days together when Mommy goes away on business.

Steig, W. *Amos and Boris*. New York: Farrar, Straus, & Giroux, 1971.
A mouse and a whale are the closest of friends. When they must separate, they never forget one another. A touchingly told story.

Stein, S. B. *A child goes to school: A storybook for parents and children together*. New York: Doubleday, 1978.
Photographically illustrated stories of a boy and girl, each of whom are going to kindergarten for the first time. During the course of the year they experience a variety of separations. Each chapter has an explanation for parents that is equally valid for teachers.

Steiner, C. *I'd rather stay with you*. New York: Seabury Press, 1965.
A little kangaroo who does not want to leave his mother's pouch is helped by his mother to go to kindergarten.

Thayer, J. *A drink for Little Red Diker*. New York: William Morrow, 1963.
A little red antelope is ready for some independence but has to convince his mother. When he manages to take a drink on his own, his mother is amazed but very proud.

Waber, E. *Ira sleeps over*. Boston: Houghton Mifflin, 1972.
When Ira sleeps over at a friend's house, they both discover that having their teddy bears makes it easier to go to sleep.

Welber, R. *Goodby, hello*. New York: Pantheon Books, 1974.
Each animal says "Goodby, mother" and hello to a new adventure. The last creature is a small boy who says "Goodby mother, hello teacher."

Wells, R. *Timothy goes to school*. New York: Dial, 1981.
On the first days of school Timothy, an endearing animal, has a hard time with Claude, the class know-it-all. Things change when he meets Violet, a true friend.

Wolde, B. *Betsy's first day at nursery school*. New York: Random House, 1976.
Betsy doubts that nursery school will be any fun, but a visit there with her mother and younger brother helps to change her mind.

School Brochures and Letters

SAMPLE PRESCHOOL BROCHURE ON ADJUSTMENT

The Phasing-In or Adjustment Period

In order to encourage a comfortable, secure adjustment to the preschool environment, all children and parents will participate in a gradual phasing-in period during the first week or so of school.

THE IMPORTANCE OF GRADUAL ADJUSTMENT

Parents, most frequently mothers, are the most important people in children's lives. The most difficult part of entering a nursery school is leaving mother. It means learning that when mother leaves, she is not gone forever.

Letting go of someone loved arouses strong feelings in everyone. Children in the preschool years are learning to cope with these feelings. Seemingly babyish behavior is a clue to these feelings. It is normal for children to express these feelings as they gradually separate from the mother and establish a tie with the teacher.

Separation also involves learning to differentiate the familiar from the strange. This growing ability to differentiate is the root of all learning, including reading.

When parents invest time and effort in the adjustment period, they promote the emotional and intellectual development of their children. They join with the staff of a nursery school in contributing to the children's happiness, the children's feelings about themselves, and their continuous growth.

Some parents think their children do not need special help to make a good start. Neither parents nor staff should take a chance.

Children will have different timetables of adjustment depending on their age, previous experience with separation, and individual reaction to change. Parents should not feel embarrassed if their child takes a little longer than the other children to adjust.

PREPARATIONS FOR THE ADJUSTMENT PERIOD

Prior to the first day of attendance or at the time of registration, parents should bring their children to the nursery school for a brief visit as an initial introduction to the school and the teachers.

Shortly before your child will enter school, it is helpful to talk to him/her about the center as a place where children go to play, learn, eat, and rest. Children need to understand clearly that they continue to live at home and that at the end of the school day, the parent will always come for them.

Parents must carefully follow the schedules for the adjustment period and the regular school term. It is vital never to disappoint children by failing to return when scheduled during the adjustment period or later when the child attends the program regularly. If prevented by unforeseen circumstances to return at the promised time, the parent should telephone the center.

It is also helpful for the parents to become better acquainted with the adjustment process by reading the literature made available by the center and by attending any meetings or conferences set up for the purpose of discussing the adjustment period.

THE ADJUSTMENT PERIOD

Toddlers

Children attending toddler groups must be given special consideration during their initial participation in the program. All mothers (or fathers or babysitters) must be prepared to remain with their children for a minimum period of one month.

During the first week of attendance, the children will come for one-half of their regularly scheduled class time. The total class register will be divided in half with half of the group attending from 10:00–10:40 and the other half attending from 10:50–11:30 A.M. The shortened schedule will assist the children in making a gradual adjustment to their playmates and their teachers.

The second and third weeks will be spent on a full-time schedule with parents in the room. The last week will be spent with the parents on the premises but not directly in the room with the children.

Preschoolers

Children attending the preschool program will be assisted in making the adjustment to their school environment by a gradual phasing-in period during the first week of school in September. For the first two days, parents will be encouraged to attend school with their children for half of their regularly scheduled time. The preschool class will be divided into two groups. Eight children will attend from 9:00–10:15 A.M. and the second half of the class will attend from 10:30–11:45 A.M. Special preparations will be made so that parents can be seated in one section of the room while the children participate in the scheduled activities.

For the next two days, parents will be on the school premises but in another room. The last day will be set up so that the parents will advise children that they are leaving but that they will return for them after work.

Children will begin their normal schedule of classes after the first week.

Kindergarten

Kindergarten children who have never attended school prior to this program will be scheduled to follow a phasing-in procedure. The period of adjustment will extend over a one-week period. Parents will be encouraged to remain with their children for two days within the classroom.

The second two days will be spent with the parents on the premises but not directly in the room. On the fifth day, the parent will tell the child that she is leaving and will return to pick him/her up after lunch. During the first few days of phasing-in the children will leave with their parents after lunch.

EXTENDED ADJUSTMENT PERIODS

Any children who demonstrate difficulty with scheduling or separation will be placed on a period of extended phasing-in. Adjustment difficulties will be discussed with parents so that they can be handled on an individualized basis according to the needs of the child. Every possible assistance will be given to facilitate this process.

Any child admitted to a program during the semester will also follow the phasing-in procedures stated above.

It is essential never to "slip away" from children, regardless of their age. This destroys their sense of trust and may lead to difficult behavior at home, as well as in the nursery school. Children should not be prevented from crying. Threats, even little ones, will not help and will increase the worry and upset.

In some cases, it may be helpful for the parent to leave a scarf or other personal belonging. Such an item may need to be left for a long time as a "comforter."

It is not necessary to push children into group activities. Parents need to know that children usually adjust to the teacher first. As a new trust relationship develops, the child becomes interested in activities and gradually makes friends with the other children in the group.

A good beginning, as well as continuing adjustment to the preschool, depends on cooperation and adjustment policies and practices. This requires open communication between parents and the center staff and a sharing in the understanding of the children. The staff of the nursery school can learn from parents just as parents can learn from the staff.

If you have any questions, please call.

SAMPLE ENTRY SCHEDULE: INFANT/TODDLER CENTER

Beginnings: A Bridge Between Home and Center

We begin the year in a slow and gradual way. In this way the new children will have as much time as they need for learning to trust the teachers. The returning children will be able to reaccustom themselves to the ways of the center and build relationships with new staff members. This is a deeply important process. It is the foundation of the whole year's experience at the center for both new and returning children. It can be accomplished well only with parents present. For this reason, we ask that parents make arrangements to spend much time at the center in the first weeks and to communicate closely with the teachers about the children's ways and feelings.

In the first week all children will come on their enrolled days for an hour and a half (see the schedule that follows for all-day, morning-only, and afternoon-only children). This abbreviated schedule will permit the staff, children, and parents to meet in very small groups to begin to get to know each other. The teachers will watch carefully as you care for your child in order to learn what your child is like and the kind of care he/she is used to. You will have an opportunity during these brief sessions to ask questions and give information. This is also an important time for the staff to get to know you and your child.

This schedule may also allow the staff to begin to make brief (no more than half an hour) home visits as a way of forging closer links between home and center. Visits will take place over a period of several weeks and will be arranged on an individual basis. If a home visit is not comfortable for you, there is no pressure to have one. Please be sure to share your thoughts about this with the head teacher.

Any questions you may have about the beginning days and the schedule can be brought up and discussed at the first parents' meeting.

Entry Schedule for Children Under Three, Full and Part Time

FIRST WEEK

Parents and children come only on days for which they are enrolled.

8:30–10:00 A.M.   Children who attend full day and their parents
11:00–12:30 A.M.   Children who attend mornings only and their parents
2:00–3:30 P.M.   Children who attend afternoons only and their parents

SECOND WEEK

Returning children will begin to move gradually toward their full hours if they are able to do so securely and comfortably. Parents' presence will vary and should be discussed with the teacher.

New children may need more time to adjust to the center and may follow their first week schedule or move slowly toward an increase in time. Please discuss these plans with the teacher.

THIRD WEEK

Each child's schedule will be planned individually within his/her enrolled days until she/he is able to attend for the fully scheduled time. Decisions will be made by teachers and parents together, based on the children's needs and capacities and the parents' needs and pressures.

SAMPLE LETTERS TO PARENTS

Dear Parents,

Welcome to the Nursery School.

You are cordially invited to the first parents' meeting of the school year to be held on Tuesday, September 14th at 8:00 P.M. in the nursery school. It will be an important and interesting meeting during which we will discuss various aspects of the school. The Board of Directors will be introduced and you will have the chance to ask any questions you may have about the school.

There also will be class meetings at which time you will have the opportunity to meet your child's teacher, see his/her classroom, and learn about plans for your child's school year.

We look forward to seeing you at the meeting and saying hello over a cup of coffee.

Sincerely yours,

President, Board of Directors

Director

Dear Parents:

School begins on _____.

_____is assigned to classroom _____, which

meets on _____ from 9:00–11:45 A.M.
1:15–4:00 P.M.

The teacher is _____.

The hours for the first day _____will be from _____ to _____. Many years of experience have shown us that children adjust better when a parent is present the first time. Please be prepared to stay at the school during this session. (Please make arrangements for your other children.) Car pools and such do not begin until the children attend a full session. Please refer to the enclosed staggered schedule. It lists the class hours for the first week of school.

The second tuition payment and all forms are due by mail September 7th.

Total tuition balance $_____

> Tuition due by mail September 7th $_____
> Next payment due November 6th $_____
> Final payment due January 22nd $_____

Please make check payable to: NURSERY SCHOOL

The following forms are due by September 7th:
1. A filled-out medical form, indicating that your child is in good health and has had the proper inoculations.
2. Child's dental form.
3. All other enclosed forms.

Also, bring along a set of clothing (underwear, shirt, pants, sweater, socks, and if possible extra sneakers), *labeled with your child's name*, to be left in school. A labeled drawstring bag will be provided by the school.

Sincerely yours,

Nursery School Director

Staggered Schedule

Morning Classes: Monday through Friday 9:00–11:45 A.M.

Thursday, September 16th	Half of the class comes 9:00–10:00 A.M. The other half comes 10:30–11:30 A.M.
Friday, September 17th	Same schedule as Thursday.
Monday, September 20th	All children come 9:00–10:30 A.M.
Tuesday, September 21st	All children come 9:00–11:00 A.M.
Wednesday, September 22nd	All children come 9:00–11:30 A.M.
Thursday, September 23rd	Regular morning classes begin 9:00–11:45 A.M.

Afternoon Classes: Tuesday and Thursday 1:15–4:00 P.M.

Thursday, September 16th	Half of the class comes 1:15–2:15 P.M.
Tuesday, September 21st	Same schedule as Thursday.
Thursday, September 23rd	All children come 1:15–2:45 P.M.
Tuesday, September 28th	All children come 1:15–3:15 P.M.
Thursday, September 30th	All children come 1:15–3:45 P.M.
Tuesday, October 5th	Regular afternoon classes begin 1:15–4:00 P.M.

References

Ainsworth, M. D. S.; Bell, S. M.; & Stayton, D. J. Infant-mother attachment and social development: "Socialization" as a product of reciprocal responsiveness to signals. In M. M. Richards (Ed.), *The integration of a child into a social world.* London: Cambridge University Press, 1974.

Ainsworth, M. D. S., & Wittig, B. A. Attachment and exploratory behavior of one year olds in a strange situation. In B. M. Foss (Ed.), *Determinants of infant behavior.* London: Methuen, 1969.

Arsenian, J. M. Young children in an insecure situation. *The Journal of Abnormal and Social Psychology,* 1943, *38,* 225–49.

Bell, S. The development of the concept of object as related to infant-mother attachment. *Child Development,* 1970, *41,* 291–311.

Berger, E. H. *Parents as partners in education.* St. Louis: C. V. Mosby Co., 1981.

Bloom-Feshbach, S.; Bloom-Feshbach, J.; & Gaughran, J. The child's tie to both parents: Separation and nursery school adjustment. *American Journal of Orthopsychiatry,* 1980, *50,* 505–21.

Bowlby, J. *Attachment and loss* (Vol. 1: *Attachment;* Vol. 2: *Separation anxiety and anger*). New York: Basic Books, 1969, 1973.

Cohen, D., & Stern, V., with Balaban, N. *Observing and recording the behavior of young children.* 3rd ed. New York: Teachers College Press, 1983.

Cohler, B. J., & Geyer, S. Psychological autonomy and interdependence within the family. In F. Walsh (Ed.), *Normal family processes.* New York: Guilford Press, 1982.

Cox, F. M., & Campbell, D. Young children in a new situation with and without their mothers. *Child Development,* 1968, *39,* 123–32.

Curry, N. E., & Tittnich, E. M. *Ready or not here we come: The dilemma of school readiness.* Rev. ed. Pittsburgh: Pittsburgh University, Arsenal Family and Children's Center, 1972. (ERIC Document No. ED 168 729)

Doris, J.; McIntyre, A.; Kelsey, C.; & Lehman, E. Separation anxiety and adjustment to nursery school. Paper presented at the 79th annual meeting of the American Psychological Association, 1971.

Erikson, E. *Childhood and society.* Rev. ed. New York: W. W. Norton, 1963.

Franklin, J. B. Conscious fathering . . . a new look at daddy. *New Frontier*, May 1983, pp. 7, 10.

Freud, A. *Normality and pathology in childhood.* New York: International Universities Press, 1965.

Furman, E. *A child's parent dies: Studies in childhood bereavement.* New Haven: Yale University Press, 1974.

Furman, R. A. Experiences in nursery school consultations. In K. Baker (Ed.), *Ideas that work with young children.* Washington, D.C.: National Association for the Education of Young Children, 1972. (Reprinted from *Young Children*, 1966, 22.)

Greenacre, P. The childhood of the artist: Libidinal phase development and giftedness. In R. Eissler, A. Freud, H. Hartmann, and E. Kris (Eds.), *The psychoanalytic study of the child*, Vol. 12. New York: International Universities Press, 1957.

Hock, E.; McKenry, P. C.; Hock, M.D.; Triolo, S.; & Stewart, L. Child's school entry: A stressful event in the lives of fathers. *Family Relations*, 1980, *29*, 467–72.

Honig, A. The young child and you—learning together. In J. F. Brown (Ed.), *Curriculum planning for young children.* Washington, D.C.: National Association for the Education of Young Children, 1982.

Jalongo, M. R. Using crisis-oriented books with young children. *Young Children*, 1983, *38*(5), 29–35.

Kaplan, L. J. *Oneness and separateness: From infant to individual.* New York: Simon & Schuster, 1978.

Katan, A. Some thoughts about the role of verbalization in early childhood. In R. S. Eissler, A. Freud, H. Hartmann, & M. Kris (Eds.), *The psychoanalytic study of the child*, Vol. 16. New York: International Universities Press, 1961.

Katz, L. The enabling model in early childhood programs. In L. Katz (Ed.), *A Collection of papers for teachers.* Urbana, Ill.: University of Illinois, 1974.

Kessler, J. W.; Ablon, G.; & Smith, E. Separation reactions in young, mildly retarded children. *Children*, 1969, *16*, 2–7.

Klaus, M. H., & Kennell, J. H. *Maternal infant bonding.* St. Louis: C. V. Mosby Co., 1976.

———. *Parent-infant bonding.* 2nd ed. St. Louis: C. V. Mosby Co., 1982.

Lamb, M. E. Fathers and child development: An integrative overview. In M. E. Lamb (Ed.), *The role of the father in child development*, 2nd ed. New York: John Wiley, 1981.

Lamb, M. E. Early contact and maternal-infant bonding: One decade later. *Pediatrics*, 1982, *70*, 763–68.

Lamb, M. E., & Hwang, C. P. Maternal attachment and mother-neonate bonding: A critical review. In M. E. Lamb & A. Brown (Eds.), *Advances in developmental psychology.* Hillsdale, N.J.: Erlbaum, 1982.

Mahler, M. S.; Pine, F.; & Bergman, A. *The psychological birth of the human infant: Symbiosis and individuation.* New York: Basic Books, 1975.

Paul, E. A study of the relationship between separation and field dependency in a group of three year old nursery school children. Master's thesis, Bank Street College of Education, 1975.

Rheingold, H. L., & Eckerman, C. O. Departures from the mother. In H. R. Schaffer (Ed.), *The origins of human social relations*. New York: Academic Press, 1971.

Resch, R. C. Separation: Natural observations in the first three years of life in an infant day care unit. Doctoral dissertation, New York University, 1975.

Rodriquez, D. T., & Hignett, W. F. Infant day care: How very young children adapt. *Children Today*, 1981, *10*, 10–12.

Schaffer, H. R., & Emerson, D. E. The development of social attachments in infancy. *Monographs of the Society for Research in Child Development*, 1964, *24*(3, serial no. 94).

Selman, R. L., & Selman, A. P. Children's ideas about friendship: A new theory. *Psychology Today*, October 1979, pp. 71–80, 114.

Small, F. "Give me to warble spontaneous songs . . .": Using spontaneity to develop a therapeutic music program. Master's thesis, Bank Street College of Education, 1983.

Speers, R. N.; McFarland, M. B.; Arnaud, S.; & Curry, N. E. Recapitulation of separation-individuation processes when the normal three-year-old enters nursery school. In J. B. McDevitt & C. F. Settlage (Eds.), *Separation-individuation: Essays in honor of Margaret S. Mahler*. New York: International Universities Press, 1971.

Weber, I. Study of development practices at Spuyten Duyvil Infantry Cooperative Nursery School. Master's thesis, Bank Street College of Education, 1959.

White, R. W. Motivation reconsidered: The concept of competence. In M. Almy (Ed.), *Early childhood play: Selected academic readings*. New York: Associated Educational Services Corp., 1968.

Winnicott, D. W. *Mother and child: A primer of first relationships*. New York: Basic Books, 1957.

Index